OUR OWN SWEET SOUNDS

Our Own Sweet Sounds

A Celebration of Popular Music in Arkansas

Second Edition

Robert Cochran

The University of Arkansas Press

Fayetteville

2005

09 08 07 06 05

5 4 3 2 1

Designed by Liz Lester

The paper used in this publication
meets the minimum requirements of
the American National Standard for
Permanence of Paper for Printed
Library Materials Z39. 48-1984.

LIBRARY OF CONGRESS
CATALOGING-IN-
PUBLICATION DATA

Cochran, Robert, 1943–
    Our own sweet sounds :
a celebration of popular music
in Arkansas / Robert Cochran.—
2nd ed.
        p.   cm.
    Includes bibliographical refer-
ences (p.   ), discography (p.   ),
and index.
    ISBN 1-55728-793-7 (pbk. :
alk. paper)
    1. Popular music—Arkansas—
History and criticism. I. Title.
    ML3477.C63   2005
    781.64'09767—dc22
                        2004028051

This project was made possible
in part by support from the Old
State House Museum and the
Arkansas Natural and Cultural
Resources Council.

FIGURE 1 Wylie Eoff and Others.
*Courtesy of Shiloh Museum of Ozark
History, Springdale*

CONTENTS

Acknowledgments

Our Own Sweet Sounds is an effort to display the community that is Arkansas as it has manifested itself in song. It began as the catalog for a 1995–1996 exhibit at the Old State House Museum in Little Rock, and has been revised and expanded to accompany the much larger 2003–2005 *Our Own Sweet Sounds II* installation at the same location.

A state is first of all an arbitrary construct, created by political fiat, empty of substance. Various flags fly over it; birds ignore its boundaries. Only with the passage of time and the shared joys and vicissitudes of life does a place on the earth become a community, a ground the heart calls home. Arkansas has long since been such a place, and music helped make it so. Even now, when Arkansas musicians achieve wider fame, it gives us pleasure to claim them as our own. If signs at the limits of several cities announce them as a president's home, similar signs at the edges of more others remind visitors that musicians were born there. Such sounds are sweet indeed. We are pleased to call them ours.

I'm grateful to Bill Gatewood, executive director of the Old State House, for asking me to serve as "guest curator" for both *Our Own Sweet Sounds* exhibits. I knew a good bit about Arkansas music, though not as much as some other people they could have asked, and not nearly as much then as I know now, having worked for most of a year on the first exhibit and maybe eighteen months on the second. The whole project was one job done over almost a decade, finally, and the work was accomplished by many people working well together. At the Old State House I worked most with Gail Moore and Jo Ellen Maack, but the exhibits also benefited greatly from the efforts of Larry Ahart, Steve Gable, Susan James, David Kennedy, Nathan Mountain, Amy Peck, Georganne Sisco, and Gerry Stoltz. Kris Katrosh and his colleagues at the Dempsey film group in Little Rock created a lovely video and designed a wonderful interactive kiosk for the second exhibit, and Larry Malley, Brian King, Liz Lester, Anna Moore, Tom Lavoie, and Debbie Self at the University of Arkansas Press have now put two editions of this catalog/history together. The time-consuming and

FIGURE 2 Patsy Montana. *Courtesy of Country Music Hall of Fame® and Museum.*

critically important task of locating photographs and securing permission for their use was accomplished with tireless efficiency by the wonderful Jo Ellen Maack (though I did have to restrain her impulse to include a tabloid shot of a spectacularly disheveled Glen Campbell, taken while the troubled ex-celebrity was in custody).

W. K. McNeil, folklorist at the Ozark Folk Center State Park in Mountain View, who surely knows more about Arkansas music than anyone alive, helpfully shared that knowledge with us at every step from initial installation of the exhibit to the preparation of this history. Lee Anthony and Bob Boyd, both of Little Rock, have been active in the Arkansas music scene for nearly half a century, and I was aided on many occasions by their generous assistance. Lovers of Arkansas music also owe gratitude to Steve Koch for his long championing of Louis Jordan and more recently for his superb *Arkansongs* radio series, and to Phillip Martin for many wonderful newspaper pieces devoted to our state's music and musicians. I've learned a great deal from both of them.

At the University of Arkansas Libraries, Carolyn Allen, Robert Bender, Anne Marie Candido, Andrea Cantrell, Debby Cochran, Ellen Compton, Michael Dabrishus, Judy Ganson, Cassandra McCraw, Rachel Reynolds, and Ethel Simpson provided valuable help. The Shiloh Museum in Springdale provided useful information and lovely photographs—thanks to Bob Besom, Susan Young, and Manon Wilson—and Magdalene Collums at the Southwest Arkansas Regional Archives at the Old Washington Historic State Park located several old photographs for us. Thanks also to the Brumley Music Company for permission to use a photograph of Albert Brumley. Mike Hoffman, George Sabo, David Sloan, and Jeannie Whayne assisted with researching the references to Indian music in the accounts of the first European visitors. Caroline Cunningham, Oscar Fendler, Willard Gatewood, Bobby Roberts, Jeannie Whayne, and Margaret Woolfolk helped locate Sadie Beck's Plantation.

I also learned from the work of current and former students: Charlie Coil (Ollie Gilbert), Elizabeth Foster ("Rock Island Line"), Courtney Hill ("Rock Island Line"), Jennifer Mathis (Forester), Lori Peterson (WPA slave narratives, Rosetta Tharpe), and Arch Schaeffer (Cate Brothers). My friend Tom Cochran let me read and use his fine article on Ronnie Hawkins, and Mike Shirkey helped me with the bluegrass bands. Thanks are due to Holly and Rudy Teaff at Fayetteville's Sound Warehouse and to Timothy Anthony at Soul Brother Records in Little Rock for generous help with the discography. I also learned much about the state's black gospel traditions from Lee Anthony. Kyle Kellams produced a segment on the exhibit for the "Ozarks at Large" program on KUAF radio in Fayetteville and got nothing for his pains but a T-shirt. Susan Pierce at the *Arkansas Democrat-Gazette* wrote a piece on the first exhibit, and Jack Hill of the same newspaper attended its opening and made a number of helpful suggestions in a review of this book's first edition. Dana Harris manages our office at the Center for Arkansas and Regional Studies, and she was as helpful and painstaking on behalf of this project as she is for everything we do.

At a more general level I want to record my gratitude to colleagues, students, friends, and fellow music lovers for loaning me tapes and CDs, inviting me to concerts, and otherwise encouraging this effort—thanks to Chuck Adams, Jim Borden, Bob Brinkmeyer, Milton Burke, David Chappell, Debra Cohen, Joel Gordon, Jacob Lewis, Susan Marren, Meredith Martin, Susan Porter, Rachel Reynolds, P. J. Robowski, Jimmie Rogers, George Sabo, Steve Smith, Alan Spurgeon, Justin Weiss, Elliott West, and Glen Wheeler. I'm grateful, too, to Dean Donald Bobbitt of the Fulbright College of Arts and Sciences at the University of Arkansas in Fayetteville, for appointing me director of the Center for Arkansas and Regional Studies, and to Provost Bob Smith and Chancellor John White for supporting the Center's work. It's the only administrative job I ever coveted; in it my work is serious play. My youngest son Taylor has met Billy Lee Riley; his big brother Jesse attended the Helena Blues Festival in a stroller; their sister Masie got a rose from Solomon Burke and owns the autograph of Larry Davis. Their mother, Suzanne, has seen it all—played hostess to Sleepy LaBeef and been smooched by an Elvis imitator.

Finally I'd like to solicit, right here at the beginning, any and all suggestions for corrections and improvements. I've tried to do a thorough job, but I had no real models. This is a first attempt, now a revised first attempt; it will still have flaws. Maybe we'll even manage a third edition. Teach me at: The Center for Arkansas and Regional Studies, Old Main 506, University of Arkansas, Fayetteville, AR 72701.

1 ✿ WITH FIDDLES AND HYMNALS

From the first, music mattered. You can see it even in what archaeologists find in the ground, in the holdings of a French museum—fragments of cane flutes and whistles older than Columbus, a man carrying a rattle (the state's earliest musician of record) on a ceremonial robe. But you can't hear it, and until the first explorers' accounts, dating from the sixteenth and seventeenth centuries, you can't even read about it. The Osage drums, the leg rattles of Caddo (and later Cherokee) dancers, the voices of Quapaws raised in song—all is silence.

Then, in the early 1540s, DeSoto came through, spending the better part of two years wandering through the state's eastern and southern regions. But there's little music in this first encounter—though the documentation is copious, what's chronicled is mostly a long and shameful record of pillage and rapine, enlivened only by vivid anecdotes of mail-clad conquistadores falling out of boats and sinking like stones forever out of sight, or fierce Indian men and women defending their homes with blows above and below Spanish belts.

Perhaps the earliest surviving reference to Arkansas music comes a bit more than a century later, from March 12, 1682, when René-Robert Cavelier, Sieur de La Salle, on his way down the Mississippi, arrived at the Quapaw village of Kappa. Greeted by the sound of singing, the Frenchmen were at first apprehensive, mistaking welcome for war-cry. But once peaceful intentions were communicated on both sides, a party was soon under way, featuring singing and dancing to the accompaniment of "gourds full of pebbles and two drums, which are earthen pots covered with dressed skin."[1]

Henri Joutel, five years later in 1687, registered his approval of a similar "concert" performed this time by Caddo hosts in southwest Arkansas for another La Salle party on the way back north from a disastrous expedition to the Texas gulf coast that cost its leader his life (murdered by two of his own men):

FIGURE 3 Shape Note Singing School. *Courtesy of Arkansas History Commission, Little Rock*

The Song was begun again, the women mixing in the chorus, and the Concert was heightened by great hollow Calabashes or Gourds, in which there were large Gravel Stones, to make a Noise, the Indians striking on them by Measure, to answer the Tone of the Choir; and the pleasantest of all was, that one of the Indians placed himself behind Monsieur Cavelier to hold him up, whilst at the same Time he shook and dandled him from Side to Side, the Motion answering to the Music.[2]

Here for once, in a journey otherwise filled with mutiny and murder, all is "Concert"—residents and visitors joined in happy celebration, the music an aural proof of welcome and amity.

Victor Tixier, however, writing a century and a half later, was less pleased by his encounter with an Osage musician who had somehow acquired "the body of a clarinet" and had made his own reed and mouthpiece:

By dint of patient studies, he succeeded in uttering three notes; but these three notes recurred constantly. Every evening our musician practiced for several hours. Those people who have had for neighbors beginner students of flageolet or cornet can imagine how pleased we were with this man.[3]

By this time settlement from the east was under way in earnest, and the Indian nations were either gone west or living in much-reduced circumstances. But early settlers in the Ozark counties, interviewed by pioneer historian Silas Turnbo in the first years of this century, still remembered Indian "green corn dances which occurred annually about roasting ear time" in the 1820s and 1830s. These were elaborate affairs involving whole communities—Turnbo in one place speaks of a one-hundred-and-fifty-foot ring of dancers. White visitors were invited to participate, but if they accepted "the Indians would make sport of their awkwardness."[4] Can't dance, can't jump—it's a scandalous libel, but it's been around for a long time.

Awkward they may have been, but they loved to dance. Early reports from Arkansas Post and the settlements along the Arkansas River reveal a pronounced attachment to musical entertainments among the early European settlers. Writing in the first years of the nineteenth century, the

Frenchman François Marie Perrin du Lac noted that the habitants of Arkansas Post devoted themselves almost entirely to hunting, instead of ostensibly more civilized agricultural pursuits. Home from the chase, they "pass their time playing games, dancing, drinking, or doing nothing."[5] James Miller, the territorial governor, also described the musical culture at Arkansas Post in unflattering terms: "They have one fiddler who can play but one tune, [and] they can dance but one figure, which is a kind of reel or cotillion."[6] The English botanist Thomas Nuttall, ascending the Arkansas River in 1819 looking for exotic New World plants, was similarly dismayed by what he encountered in the frontier settlements, noting that the "love of amusements, particularly gambling and dancing parties or balls," was "carried to extravagance" among the inhabitants.[7]

The geologist George W. Featherstonhaugh, traveling in the southwestern corner of the territory in 1834, was harshly critical of nearly everything he saw of frontier society (though he found Hot Springs a geologist's paradise), but even he was astonished and impressed to find "a piano in the wilderness" at the home of one of his hosts near the Arkansas Washington, in Hempstead County.[8]

Less than ten years later, up in the Ozarks, the German adventurer Friedrich Gerstäcker was also encountering music both secular and sacred in the isolated mountain settlements. When a Methodist meeting at one home began when the minister "thundered out a hymn with a voice that astounded me," Gerstäcker had little idea that the "singing and praying" would continue for hours, until "I was heartily tired of it, for it did not agree with my habits and feelings." More to his liking was a July 4 "frolic" near Fourche le Fave where dancers, knowing both their own need for music and the musicians' need for strong drink, planned accordingly and reserved the services of more than one fiddler. The first went down early in the evening after profanely expressing "a most disagreeable wish respecting the eyes of all the company, on account of the dryness of his throat, which had only had the contents of two bottles of whisky down it." His usefulness thus ended, the musician was "seized by the arms and legs, and unceremoniously carried out." The second fiddler lasted until midnight, but then he too faltered and "was carried out and laid on the grass while a third was soon found to take his place."[9]

Featherstonhaugh, back in Little Rock from his wanderings to Hot Springs and the Texas border in 1834, described a more urbanized if hardly more urbane celebration. A Christmas Eve "ball" held in a tavern featured "about 100 men and three women" in which "the men had their hats on, and danced armed with pistols and bowie knives." Liquor flowed freely at this affair, so that by its close "the whole party soon got amazingly drunk, but were very good-natured, 'for there were only a few shots fired in fun.'"[10]

The name of Arkansas was by this time becoming familiar to Americans from other regions—it was "the creation state, the finishing-up country—a state where the *sile* runs down to the centre of the 'arth," in Thomas Bangs Thorpe's "The Big Bear of Arkansas," first published in 1841. Herman Melville's image of the state, however, was less complimentary and more typical—the maddened Captain Ahab, attacking a whale with a jackknife in *Moby Dick,* is described as "like an Arkansas duelist," while the English traveler and author Frederick Marryat told London readers in 1858 that Arkansas court dockets were loaded with "more cases of stabbing and looting than ten of the other States put together."[11]

The musical companion to all this was of course the "Arkansas Traveler." Its origins remain mysterious, but by 1845 it was known as a fiddle tune, and in 1849 it was reported as the name of a racehorse and the most popular dance tune in Hot Springs. As a humorous dialogue it was in print by 1860, and in 1869 a drama entitled *Kit the Arkansas Traveler* opened in Buffalo and held the stage until the end of the century. Two paintings by Arkansan Edward P. Washbourne, *The Arkansas Traveler* and *The Turn of the Tune,* were published to wide popularity as Currier and Ives engravings in 1870. The song, the dialogue, the drama, the engravings—taken together they made "The Arkansas Traveler" famous. It was, said its most thorough student, "the most celebrated specimen of Arkansas folklore and humor."[12]

The basic story is simplicity itself: a solitary traveler approaches an isolated Arkansas cabin on horseback; in the doorway the homesteader plays the first part of a jig called "The Arkansas Traveler" over and over. The fiddler responds rudely to several queries—this constitutes the humorous dialogue—but when the traveler offers to play the tune's second part, or "turn," he's suddenly offered the warmest of hospitality.

The lesson is clear, functioning here much as it did for the party of Frenchmen hosted by the Caddo a century and a half earlier: music makes welcome, establishes amity. The guest who can sing (or play) for his supper will eat well. The tune was on record early—a 1902 version by Len Spencer on Edison may be the first. Finally, in 1922, "The Arkansas Traveler" and "Sally Goodin" were paired on what is often cited as the first country music record—Henry Gilliland and Arkansas-born "Eck" Robertson performing on fiddles.[13]

FIGURE 4 *The Arkansas Traveler*, painted by Edward Payson Washbourne. *Courtesy of Special Collections Division, University of Arkansas Libraries, Fayetteville*

There were several other songs about Arkansas in circulation by the end of the nineteenth century, though none approached "The Arkansas Traveler" in popularity. "The State of Arkansas" is the lament of a working man (often named Bill Stafford or Sanford Barnes) who "never knowed what misery was / Till I come to Arkansas." Arriving by train in Hot Springs (or, less often, Little Rock) he is conducted by its owner to the self-proclaimed best hotel in Arkansas, where he's fed on corn dodger and "beef I could not chaw." He works hard—on railroads or at clearing and draining land—but is so poorly paid and fed that after six weeks (or months) he's planning on moving further west "to the Nation" where he hopes to "marry me a squaw." His last words are a promise never to return.[14]

"Down in Arkansas" (or "Down in the Arkansas") is another comic ditty, written by the vaudeville comedian George "Honeyboy" Evans and first published in 1913. There's no narrative, and the song is best remembered today for its chorus, but there are several self-contained verses—one tells of a man who took his cow to the vet because it "slobbered bad." The doc's advice: "Teach that cow to spit." A third song, also comic, is commonly titled "The Arkansas Boys" or "The Arkansas Run." This one warns Missouri (or Tennessee) girls against falling for boys from Arkansas, whose many shortcomings the song details. They wear ridiculous clothes ("A old white hat without no crown, / An' old blue duckins the whole year round"), eat poor food ("Cornbread an' possum an' sassafras tea"), and live in tumbledown shacks ("Stick-an'-clay chimney, old dirt floor, / Clapboard roof an' a batten door"). Marry such a man and all this will be yours—"Some gets a little an' some gets none, / An' that's the way of the Arkansas run."[15]

All these songs are commonly found in folk-song collections, their authorship is characteristically unknown or (in the case of "Down in Arkansas") forgotten, and they have circulated in widely varying forms under several titles. But professional songwriters were also on the scene early in Arkansas. A "Fayetteville Polka," written by Fayetteville music teacher Ferdinand Zellner and reportedly inspired by the accomplishments of his students at Miss Sophie Sawyer's Female Seminary, was published in the 1850s, while Eva Ware Barnett's "Arkansas," printed in Little Rock in 1916, includes a celebration of the state's mineral resources: "'Tis a land full of joy and sunshine, / Rich in pearls and in diamonds rare."

But surely Arkansas's strangest song from this period is "My Happy Little Home in Arkansas," written for distribution at the Columbian Exposition in Chicago in 1893 by Henry DeMoss. This is a thoroughly commercial effort by a professional songwriter—DeMoss, who led a traveling family of musical entertainers who called Oregon home, wrote Columbian songs for every state—but it became very popular in the state in the years just after the exposition. Many children learned it in school, knowledge of its origins was often lost, and by 1904 it had been published as an anonymous folk song. The song is largely forgotten now, but the University of Arkansas folk-song collection has a 1950s recording by Doney Hammontree.

The music of African American Arkansans is also a part of the early accounts. Featherstonhaugh, for example, in the account of his 1834 journey, includes a "Comical relation of a solo played by a Negro to a Gang of Wolves," the story of Mr. Marcus Luffett, "a black man . . . who played on the fiddle" who was summoned to a merrymaking at new year . . . to play 'Virginia reels' to the young people." The party lasts until three in the morning, but Mr. Luffett's adventures are only then beginning. On his way home he is pursued by a gang of wolves but manages not only to escape into an abandoned cabin but also to trap thirty-seven wolves inside by climbing into the rafters and closing the door from above. Afraid to summon help before daylight by escaping through a hole in the roof, he stayed in the rafters and "commenced with his kit to astonish the lupine auditory with such a solo as they had never heard before." Featherstonhaugh does not record what Luffett was paid for his fiddling, but for trapping the wolves he got all the skins and "the neighbors subscribed twenty-five dollars in cash."[16]

Spencer Polk, who lived from 1833 until 1919, was the son of a white father and black mother in Howard County. He raised his own large family in a complex hybrid culture that may have been unusual in its own day but in some ways anticipates more widespread future interactions. His granddaughter's study of the family's life focuses at one point on the music:

> In addition to their folklore, everyday practices, and beliefs, the Polks enjoyed a musical tradition that represented a cultural mix of slave seculars and Scottish ditties. On the one hand, the family

passed on chants and songs that were popular among Afro-Americans and which no doubt had an African-American origin. On the other hand, the Polks actively participated in the musical tradition of the whites in the Muddy Fork community, with the Polk women attending the square dances and the male members of the family providing the music and "calling" the sets. . . .

Spencer's son Arthur had a beautiful tenor voice, and the members of the household always knew when things were going well, for Arthur walked around singing folksongs and doing his Scotch-Irish version of a popular Afro-American musical innovation called "scat." Two of Arthur's favorite songs were "Cindy" and "Sally Good'n."[17]

It's wonderful to be able to read the story of Spencer Polk and his family, but most people don't have articulate and determined children or grandchildren, and their stories get told less fully, or not told at all. Many black Arkansans, however, did find their own voice in the extraordinary interviews that make up *The American Slave: A Composite Autobiography.* Gathered by the Arkansas Federal Writers Project under WPA sponsorship from 1936 until 1939 under the capable direction of Bernice Babcock and a cadre of dedicated interviewers both black and white, the Arkansas narratives are the crowning glory of the collection, "not only the largest but the richest in terms of content."[18] Its more than one thousand manuscript pages are filled with indications of music's importance. It may not be surprising to hear in the recollections of people who were often worked from "sun to sun" or "can see to can't see" memories of songs associated with work. John Patterson of Helena, born in Kentucky but brought to Arkansas by his mother at the age of four "to be kept from the Yankee soldiers," recalled snatches of "plough songs" and remembered singing as a feature of the closing hours of the workday: "About four o'clock we all start up singing. Sing till dark."[19] Rose Adway of Pine Bluff recited three verses of "Climbing Jacob's Ladder" and remembered where she learned them: "My mother used to sing dat when she was spinnin' and cardin'."[20]

But work was not all, not by half. John Cottonham, born in Lake Village in 1866, remembered "one solid month" each year, when slaves would "go on a month's spree of dancing, eating and drinking. This was

at Varner, on Bob Rice's place, you know he was one of the big sportin' men."[21] According to Mrs. Cora Gillam of Little Rock, "colored folks had parties as well as the white folks. On our place, the slaves had a regular band: fiddler, banjo player, tambourine player. They played any kind of song. They would play for the dances."[22] Mary Ann Brooks of Pine Bluff was proud of being "a mighty dancer when I was young," and told of one night when "paddyrollers run us home from dancin'."[23]

A number of musicians who played for such gatherings were also interviewed. "I'm a musician, played the fife," said Jeff Davis of Pine Bluff. "Played it to a T. Had two kinds of drums. Had different kinds of brass horns too. I 'member one time they was a fellow thought he could beat the drum till I took it." James Davis, also of Pine Bluff, was no less proud of his skills: "I used to be one of the best banjo pickers. I was good. Played for white folks and called figgers for 'em. In them days they said 'promenade,' 'sashay,' 'swing corners.'"[24]

Sam Scott of Russellville listed "show business" as his main occupation: "Yes, I still takes out a show occasionally to de towns around Pope and Yell and Johnson counties, and folks treat us mighty fine. Big crowds—played to $47.00 clear money at Clarksville. Usually take about eight and ten in our comp'ny, boys and gals—and we give 'em a real hot minstrel show."[25]

References to church services and hymn singing are also found throughout the narratives. "Aunt Adeline" of Fayetteville, up in the Ozark country where farms were smaller and slaves fewer, remembered earning money for the first time when stagecoach passengers overheard her "playing church" with her master's daughter and rewarded the girls' hymn singing with a dime.[26] Lucretia Alexander of Little Rock had less benign memories—she recalled slaves holding secret church services on weekday evenings where worshipers "used to sing their songs in a whisper and pray in a whisper."[27]

Memories of the Civil War have a prominent place in the slave narratives, with occasional references to songs reflecting sympathy with each side. "There wasn't no fightin' in Union County," recalled Katie Arbery, "but I 'member when the Yankees was goin' through and singin'

"The Union forever, hurrah, boys, hurrah
We'll rally 'round the flag, boys,
Shouting the battle cry of freedom."[28]

Rachel Bradley of Pine Bluff, however, sang a good bit of a southern song for her interviewer:

Homespun dresses plain I know
And the hat palmetto too.
Hurrah! Hurrah!
We cheer for the South we love so dear,
We cheer for the homespun dresses
The Southern ladies wear!

Who is Price a fightin'?
He is a fightin', I do know.
I think it is old Curtis,
I hear the cannons roa'.[29]

Another song reflecting southern sympathies was remembered by Maria Clements of De Valls Bluff:

Jeff Davis is President
Abe Lincoln is a fool
Come here, see Jeff ride the gray horse
And Abe Lincoln the mule.[30]

It is fair to say, however, despite such instances, that slave sympathies were overwhelmingly with the Union forces—more than one male interviewee recalled going to the war as a servant to a Confederate master, but leaving for the Union side at the first opportunity. Ellen Brass of Little Rock, for example, was in Louisiana during the war, but she recalled that "it wasn't the white folks on the plantation that told us we was free. It was the soldiers their selves that came around and told us. We called 'em Yankees. . . . They had us all out in the yard dancing and playing. They sang the song:

They hung Jeff Davis on a sour apple tree

While we all go marching on.[31]

Yet another outstanding example of pro-Union African American music from Arkansas's Civil War period is the 1863 "Song of the First of Arkansas," a marching song written especially for the "First Arkansas Colored Regiment" by Lindley Miller, who was evidently a member of the unit. The song opens in statement of purpose and assertion of military prowess—"We are fightin' for de Union, we are fightin' for de law; / We can hit a rebel furder dan a white man eber saw"—but then moves on to stress the effects of the just-issued Emancipation Proclamation. "We heard de proclamation, massa hush it as he may," says a later stanza, adding that masters will now "hab to pay us wages" and "bow their foreheads to their colored kith and kin."[32]

Almost any soldier's memoir from the period will do to demonstrate the importance of music to Arkansas soldiers. Captain John W. Lavender's account of his experiences as commander of Company F of the Fourth Arkansas Infantry, enrolled at Mount Ida in 1861, includes a mention of "Our Band of Music"—evidently a fife and drum corps that used homemade drums and "Fife made from [joints] of cane." Lavender was captured in 1864, and his account of the Confederate prison train's encounter with a "large fat German" civilian in the Indianapolis train station is a highlight of the memoir:

> One large fat German wanted to Kill the hole lot of us. Some of the Boys Jawed him and he Rushed in over the line and aboute a Dozen of us got ahold of him. The gard Said, Boys don't hurt him, have all the fun you want to with him. . . . We over Powered him, got him up on our Shoulders and marched up and Down under the Shed and sang Dixie and several Southern war songs. He was so mad he Frothed at the Mouth.[33]

Reminiscences of a Private, the memoir of Confederate soldier William E. Bevens, provides a wonderful anecdote indicating the importance of music in the Civil War camps. Soldiers were so devoted to dancing that they "tied handkerchiefs on the arms of the smallest boys to take the part of ladies in making up square dances."[34]

SONG

OF THE

FIRST OF ARKANSAS.

The following song was written by Captain Lindley Miller, of the First Arkansas Colored Regiment. Captain Miller says the "boys" sing the song on dress parade with an effect which can hardly be described, and he adds that "while it is not very conservative, it will do to fight with." Captain Miller is a son of the late ex-Senator Miller, of New Jersey.

Oh! we're de bully soldiers of de "First of Arkansas,"
We are fightin' for de Union, we are fightin' for de law;
We can hit a rebel furder dan a white man eber saw,
   As we go marching on.
   Glory, glory, hallelujah, &c.

See dar! above de centre, where de flag is wavin' bright;
We are goin' out of slavery; we are bound for freedom's light;
We mean to show Jeff. Davis how the Africans can fight,
   As we go marching on.

We hab done wid hoein' cotton, we hab done with hoein' corn,
We are colored Yankee soldiers now, as sure as you are born;
When de Massas hear us yellin' dey'll tink its Gabriel's horn,
   As we go marching on.

Dey will hab to pay us wages, de wages ob their sin,
Dey will hab to bow their foreheads to their colored kith and kin,
Dey will hab to gib us house-room, or de roof shall tumble in,
   As we go marching on.

We heard de proclamation, massa hush it as he will;
De bird he sing it to us, hoppin on de cotton hill,
And de possum up de gum tree he couldn't keep it still,
   As he went climbing on.

Dey said, "Now colored bredren, you shall be forever free,
From the first of January, eighteen hundred and sixty-three;
We heard it in de riber goin' rushin' to de sea,
   As it went sounding on,

Father Abraham has spoken, and de message has been sent,
De prison doors he opened, and out de pris'ners went,
To join de sable army of de "Afrian descent,"
   As we go marching on.

Den fall in colored bredren, you'd better do it soon,
Don't you hear de drum a beatin' de Yankee Doodle tune?
We are wid you now dis mornin', we'll be far away at noon,
   As we go marching on.

Published by the Supervisory Committee for Recruiting Colored Regiments

FIGURE 5 "Song of the First of Arkansas" (1863). *Courtesy of Old State House Museum Collections, Little Rock*

Vance Randolph's great Ozark folk-song collection includes forty-three songs in the section devoted to "Songs of the Civil War," noting that even in the 1940s the singing of such songs came "uncomfortably close to the still existing feuds and family hatreds" associated with the war.[35] Arkansas's position as a border state, with divided loyalties and strong feelings on both sides, is clearly reflected in the songs themselves. "The Bonnie Blue Flag," for example, sung for Randolph in 1914 in Batesville, is credited to "Harry Macarthy, the Arkansas Comedian," and listed as second only to "Dixie" as "the most popular of the Confederate battlesongs." "I'm a Good Old Rebel," a favorite of Cane Hill singer Booth Campbell, who sang it for Randolph in 1942, is likewise clear in its southern loyalties:

> I'm glad I'm a good old rebel,
>
> I don't care if I am,
>
> I won't be reconstructed,
>
> If I am may I be damn![36]

"Babylon Is Falling" and "The Year of Jubelo," however, two songs sympathetic to the Union cause, were sung in Arkansas in the 1860s, according to Randolph's informant. Both were written by the prolific composer Henry Clay Work in the so-called "Negro dialect" popular at the time, and the latter closes with a wry and poignant celebration of the end of slavery as embodied in the hasty departure of "Old Massa" upon the appearance of "Linkum gunboats" on the river:

> The whip is lost an' the handcuffs busted,
>
> Old Massa's got his pay,
>
> He's big 'nough an' old 'nough, he orter know better
>
> Than to went and run away.[37]

Long before the Civil War, however, the musical traditions of Anglo-American settlers had been successfully transplanted to Arkansas. Everything from English and Scottish ballads to Irish fiddle tunes and Methodist hymns was being sung and played in the new territory. Ballads in particular were often carried in family traditions, and by the 1870s several

FIGURE 6 Emma Dusenbury and Her Daughter Ora, circa 1935. *Courtesy of Special Collections Division, University of Arkansas Libraries, Fayetteville*

families who would soon produce famous ballad singers were in Arkansas: Emma Dusenbury came to Baxter County in 1873; Ollie Gilbert's mother, Mary Ballentine, came to Stone County from Tennessee in the same decade; Almeda Riddle's great-grandfather was here even earlier. "My father was born and reared in White County and Cleburne County, Arkansas," she said, "and his grandfather settled this little town called Jamestown in close to Batesville."[38]

Beginning in the 1920s, folk-song collectors would record hundreds upon hundreds of songs from these women and from a multitude of other musicians and singers throughout the state. They would end up in Washington, at the Library of Congress Archive of American Folksong where more than one hundred recordings of Emma Dusenbury are housed, in university or public library collections like those at the University of Arkansas in Fayetteville or the Springfield, Missouri, public library, which holds Max Hunter's recordings of more than three hundred songs by Ollie Gilbert.

By this time, too, the state had produced its first fully professional musical "star." Essie Whitman, who was born in Osceola in 1882, toured first with her mother and sister singing jubilee songs and later as one of the Whitman Sisters on the vaudeville circuit. By 1902 she was doing European shows; by 1921 she was making records. The Whitman Sisters, wrote jazz historians Jean and Marshall Stearns, were "the royalty of Negro vaudeville."[39] Another professional from this same period was Carl Davis, a guitarist and piano player born in 1886 in Rison. He played in New Orleans with the Papa Celestin Band around 1910, toured with southern carnivals in the 1920s and 1930s, and finally got recorded by Vocalion with the Dallas Jamboree Jug Band in 1935.

FIGURE 7 Hope Cornet Band, 1885. *Courtesy of Southwest Arkansas Regional Archives, Washington, Arkansas*

But folk singers recorded by scholars are the exception, not the rule, and few professional musicians emerged from the Arkansas frontier. For this period the point most to be stressed is the abiding local base of Arkansas music. Musicians played for themselves, their families, and their neighbors in their own homes, churches, and communities. In a region visited only rarely by professional entertainers they relied mostly upon themselves, using first their own ballad singers and fiddlers and guitar players, and later creating their own church choirs and quartets, their own town cornet bands and dance orchestras. The most successful were sometimes paid—itinerant teachers taught the rudiments of harmony, often from "shape note" songbooks, in "singing schools" in churches and schools, and the most affluent citizens of the region's towns were able at surprisingly early dates to obtain lessons in piano and voice for their children. But more often than not, Arkansas music was a do-it-yourself job, an amateur affair in the best sense of the word. The homesteader in the "Arkansas Traveler" may not have known "the turn of the tune" prior to the traveler's arrival, but he had his own fiddle and he knew how to play. His descendants still do.

The frontier years were mostly a thing of the past by the 1870s—Arkansas had been a full-fledged state since 1836, after all. But still there were occasional flashes of the old rowdiness, the days when state congressmen had at each other with Bowie knives on the floor of the legislature and prominent citizens and gubernatorial candidates engaged in

FIGURE 8 Cornet Band, Jonesboro, circa 1915. *Courtesy of Special Collections Division, University of Arkansas Libraries, Fayetteville*

elaborate duels on Arkansas River sandbars. Up in Osceola, for instance, the local newspaper reported on an 1870s picnic: "After eats, gander pulling was engaged in. Mr. W. P. Hale succeeded in pulling in twain the gander's breathing apparatus, after which dancing was resumed."[40] Dancing was resumed—that's the important thing, after all, no matter the interruption, the gravity or triviality of its claims. Take care of business, says the emerging Arkansas credo, whether business is hunting, fighting Civil War battles, or throttling a goose, and get back to the dancing.

FIGURE 9 Pocahontas Cornet Band. *Courtesy of Shiloh Museum of Ozark History, Springdale*

2 ✿ RADIOS AND PHONOGRAPHS

Engineering students and professors at the University of Arkansas in Fayetteville had been experimenting with radio since the 1890s, but the story of radio broadcasting in Arkansas begins in Pine Bluff, where a three-month license to operate a 500-watt station was granted by the U.S. Department of Commerce to the local division of the Arkansas Light and Power Company (now AP&L) on February 16, 1922. It was called WOK (Workers of Kilowatts) and its first broadcast, two days later on February 18, included results of a high school basketball game.

By February 21, however, with a new transmitter in place, WOK went on the air with a two-hour concert featuring Kueck's Orchestra of Pine Bluff, and by March had added a second local band, Baim's Novelty Five, to their talent list. But before this, on February 25 no less a star than "Miss Lenora Sparks, Metropolitan Opera soprano," in town for a concert, agreed to make her first radio appearance. She sang three songs— "Smilin' Through," "Morning," and "My Curly Headed Baby."[1]

Other stations were soon licensed—by 1925 Little Rock, Fort Smith, Hot Springs, and Fayetteville were all on the air. Music dominated the programming schedule, accounting for more than 60 percent of broadcast time nationwide in the 1920s. Much of this music, moreover, was performed by local musicians, who often played music traditional to the area. Pine Bluff's WOK, for example, broadcast a program by "oldtime fiddler A. J. Matthews" in March 1923, which included "Chicken Crowed for a Day" and "Somebody Ran Away with Dinah." Matthews also reminisced on the air—he'd "played for dances near England, Arkansas, in 1892" where on at least one occasion "thirty-six couples had danced for twelve hours."[2] This sounds much like the fare presented on the several "barn dance" programs that the national networks were carrying by 1925—the *National Barn Dance* on WLS in Chicago opened in 1924, with the *WSM Barn Dance,* forerunner of the *Grand Ole Opry,* beginning in 1925. Closer to home, the *Louisiana Hayride* was carried on KWKH in

FIGURE 10 Patsy Montana's boots. *Courtesy of Old State House Museum Collections, Little Rock*

Shreveport, Louisiana, beginning in 1948, and station KWTO in Springfield, Missouri, eventually produced more than 150 shows per week, first on radio and later on television, eventually including nationally syndicated programs featuring Red Foley, Tennessee Ernie Ford, and the Carter Family.

In Little Rock, station WSV's opening program on April 8, 1922, included music by Dale's Blue Melody Boys, a five-man jazz orchestra, while Fort Smith's 5ACW (later WCAC) billed a program of the same month by Waymon Griffin's Orchestra as "the first colored orchestra to broadcast in the state."[3] In May 1923, Fayetteville station KFDV carried music by Dick Grabiel's Arkansas Travelers from a fraternity dance party—songs included "Rose of the Rio Grande," "Blues My Naughty Sweetie Gave to Me," and "Bessie Couldn't Help It"—while the same town's KFMQ in 1924 featured old-time fiddlers contests and a concert by the Black Diamond Serenaders, a hometown "Negro string orchestra."[4]

But perhaps the most influential early station in Arkansas was KTHS in Hot Springs. Within weeks of its first broadcast on December 20, 1924, the station featured a wide array of musical talent—everything from the "old-fashioned waltzes" of the ten-piece Meyer Davis Orchestra and "hoedown tunes and French harp selections" by Luke and Mack Hignite to "novelty music" by one Tin Can Joe, who evidently took his name from the instrument he played. Also appearing were the Central College Girls Glee Club from Conway, the College of the Ozarks Trio from Clarksville, and Ms. Ella Goodrow from Lonoke, composer of the hit waltz "Always You're Near.'"[5] Before the year was out a vaudeville comedian from Little Rock named Benjamin "Whitey" Ford had made his debut—behind him was a Dixieland group called Benny Ford and His Arkansas Travelers and ahead of him was a long career as the Duke of Paducah on the *Renfro Valley Barn Dance* and the *Grand Ole Opry*.

By allowing such a multitude of performers to appear, KTHS was bound to discover some real talent. When a local bank teller from Harmony Grove named Ross Graham won the Atwater Kent song contest in 1927, it was the first step in a career that would take him to New York by the early 1930s, where he would join "Roxy's Gang," an ensemble that "broadcast over NBC and performed in the music hall shows at Radio City." And when Chester Lauck and Norris Goff, two young businessmen from Mena, decided to abandon their blackface act in favor of a comedy routine featuring "two old rural characters" when they appeared on a KTHS flood relief show in 1931, who could have guessed that it would be the beginning of the nationally famous "Lum and Abner" skits?[6]

But by the 1930s radio's days as a novelty were over. There were stations in every section of the state—KBTM in Paragould (and later Jonesboro), KELD in El Dorado, KCMC in Texarkana, KOTN in Pine Bluff in 1934. Helena's KFFA would start later, in 1941, but one day it would be world famous among music lovers for a little fifteen-minute show called "King Biscuit Time."

All these stations played music, lots of music, both live and recorded. KOTN's first day's schedule included fifteen-minute shows by the True Gospel Singers (at 1:45 P.M.) and Muldoon's Syncopaters (at 5:00), while KBTM carried programs by the local Potter's Orchestra of Paragould plus regular shows featuring "Dizzy" Jack Morgan, a blind pianist and saxophonist, and Earl Carpenter, who called himself "The Boy from Back Home" and sang "hillbilly and western" songs to his own guitar accompaniment. In 1934 the station moved to nearby Jonesboro, where by 1935 it had its own *KBTM Barn Dance*, and in 1936 carried several segments from the town's fall festival, including a thirty-minute old fiddler's contest and a full-hour concert by Jack Johnson's Aristocrats of Rhythm, a "14-piece Negro Orchestra."[7]

Down in Little Rock, meanwhile, a no less varied musical menu was available on WCBN (later KLRA)—everything from a barn dance program, the *Barnyard Frolic,* to "old time religious songs" by the Antioch Choir and a program by the Jewish Temple Choir. There was also popular fare from Ted Dougan's Arkansas Razorbacks and "Miss Mona Todd, blues singer," the latter including "Ding Dong Daddy from Dumas" among her selections.[8]

While shows patterned on the national barn dances like the *Grand Ole Opry* usually lasted an hour or more and featured several musical groups and soloists as well as comic acts, the local shows usually lasted only fifteen minutes, with one performer or group appearing for a single sponsor. By the 1930s such shows were a staple of radio music. Up in the state's northwest corner western swing fiddler Frankie Kelly has been entertaining local audiences for more than half a century now, performing with his Western

Swingsters band Thursday nights at the Springdale VFW, though by 1993 his fame had spread so widely that he was inducted into the Western Swing Hall of Fame in Sacramento, California. But he got his start in 1938, at sixteen, when his Arkansas Playboys appeared regularly on a fifteen-minute noontime radio show in Fayetteville. Johnny Cash found even wider fame, and much greater fortune, but he too started out on radio. He was still an appliance salesman in early 1955 when his boss at the Home Equipment Company in Memphis agreed to sponsor a 2:00–2:15 gospel show every Saturday on KWEM in West Memphis.

But by far the most famous of such shows was the 12:15–12:30 "King Biscuit Time" show on Helena's KFFA. The station opened in November 1941, and by December had agreed to broadcast a blues music show sponsored by the local Interstate Grocery Company to promote their flour. The show, featuring guitarist Robert Lockwood and harmonica player Aleck "Rice" Miller, who billed himself as Sonny Boy Williamson, was an immediate hit, drawing one thousand fan letters each week, according to the recollections of station owner Sam Anderson, and the Interstate Grocery Company was soon selling Sonny Boy Corn Meal and setting up personal appearances by Lockwood and Williamson at grocery stores all over the region. Robert Palmer's *Deep Blues* offers a detailed portrait of the show's daily operation:

> The routine varied little from show to show. A few minutes before noon, Miller and Lockwood would arrive at the Floyd Truck Lines building, a two-story composite of wood and brick with the trucking company's loading docks on the first floor and the KFFA studios upstairs. . . . The first words, spoken with great gusto, were the announcer's: "Pass the biscuits, 'cause it's King Biscuit Time!" Miller and Lockwood would immediately launch into the show's theme, a jump-tempo blues. . . .

The show consisted of songs by Sonny Boy and Robert, many requested in cards and letters sent in by listeners, and florid commercials, read by the announcer, that were the work of Interstate's Max Moore. "Light as air! White as snow! Yes, friends, that's King Biscuit Flour, the perfect flour for all your baking."[9]

Lockwood and Williamson worked six months as a duo, but in June

1942, drummer James "Peck" Curtis was added to the show. He had been on radio before, in Blytheville, but he found a long-term home on KFFA, eventually doing more King Biscuit shows than any other performer. Pianist Robert "Dudlow" Taylor was another early addition, and over the years the King Biscuit show featured an informal Who's Who of area blues musicians: guitarists Houston Stackhouse, Joe Willie Wilkins, Willie Moore, W. C. Clay, and Herbert Wilson; Mississippi-born pianists Joe Willie "Pinetop" Perkins and Willie Love.

FIGURE 11 "King Biscuit Time" (promotional photo sent to fans of Helena station KFFA's "King Biscuit Time" show by the sponsoring Interstate Grocery Company); *from left:* Sonny Boy Williamson, announcer Sam Anderson, Robert Lockwood. *Courtesy of Arkansas History Commission, Little Rock*

The success of King Biscuit did not go unnoticed, and a sort of "flour war" soon developed on KFFA, with blues shows sponsored by at least three competing brands. By 1943 slide guitar ace Robert McCollum (born in Helena, November 30, 1909), who had made records in Chicago as Robert Nighthawk, was on the air courtesy of Bright Star Flour, and in 1945 Robert Lockwood quit the blues of King Biscuit for a jazzier show sponsored by yet another flour, Mother's Best. But "King Biscuit Time" was the first, and the most enduring. It lasted with live music until 1969, stayed on the air with records until 1980, and then was revived by local blues fans in 1986, the inaugural year of a King Biscuit Blues Festival that's still going strong.

Sonny Boy Williamson's subsequent career has made him a famous name to blues and R&B fans, but his partner Robert Lockwood was no less influential. Born in 1915 near Marvell, Lockwood first learned to play a pump organ at his grandparent's home, but was converted by the famous bluesman Robert Johnson, who came to court Lockwood's mother and taught him guitar so well that he was known locally as Robert Jr. Lockwood in simultaneous recognition of the teacher's mastery and the student's aptitude. In the 1930s Lockwood, having played in Elaine, was told upon his return to Helena that Johnson had arrived in Elaine. He went back, only to find that "it wasn't until I got back down there that I realized that man had done come and looked at me playing and got me going back down there looking for myself."[10]

But great as Johnson's influence was, Lockwood continued to develop his own skills, and these took new directions after Johnson's death in 1938. By 1941, when he started working on KFFA, Lockwood was playing an electric guitar and listening avidly to Count Basie and Benny Goodman. He was, notes Palmer, ready "to play a crucial if largely unsung role in modernizing Delta blues."[11] Lockwood was still going strong as the new millennium dawned, headlining at the Helena Blues Festival in 2002.

The example of a show like "King Biscuit Time," coupled with a look at broadcast schedules from various stations across the state, makes it clear that, very far from causing the extinction or decline of local music traditions in favor of recorded music dominated by professionals from outside the region, radio in fact stimulated local music by not only offering its makers opportunities to perform for wider audiences but also by allowing them to hear and be influenced by a wider variety of music than had previously been possible. For every Lenora Sparks from the New York Metropolitan Opera, there were scores, even hundreds of "Dizzy" Jack Morgans and Earl Carpenters, Black Diamond Serenaders and Dale's Blue Melody Boys. And what's more, when traditional performers heard new things over the radio or on records, they were anything but overwhelmed. They simply added what they liked to what they'd been doing before, fitting new songs to known forms. In fact, noted scholar Kenneth Goldstein, the process had been going on for a long time—radio had stimulated traditional music in the 1920s and 1930s just as the invention of moveable type and metal engraving in the fifteenth and sixteenth centuries "resulted in a revival to which the printing of broadsides, chapbooks, and songsters contributed greatly." Each new technological development has "supplemented rather than replaced, reinforced rather than displaced, fed rather than swallowed, the oral tradition."[12]

FIGURE 12 Robert Lockwood. *Reproduced by permission of Getty Images*

But if Arkansas musicians found it an easy matter to adapt what they learned from radio and records to what they'd been doing before, and found it easy moreover to get themselves on the air, they also found that making their own records was a more difficult matter to arrange. Commercial recording of traditional and popular music developed along with radio in the early 1920s. Mamie Smith's recording of "Crazy Blues" on the OKeh label in 1920 is often cited as the first commercial blues record, with Arkansas native Alexander "Eck" Robertson's recordings of "The Arkansas Traveler" and "Sally Gooden" with Oklahoman Henry Gilliland in 1922 the usual nominee for first commercial country music record.[13] Various titles have been touted as the earliest gospel record (as opposed to more broadly religious tunes, which were recorded much earlier), but Homer Rodeheaver, who replaced Fred Fischer as the gospel singer for Billy Sunday's evangelistic revivals in 1910, would seem to have as good a claim as any. Rodeheaver's Rainbow Records, established in 1916, was "probably . . . the first gospel label, although there is some evidence that suggests James Vaughan, in Lawrenceburg, Tennessee, may have been responsible for the first gospel recordings."[14]

The 1920s also saw the emergence of the so-called territory bands that developed the blues, ragtime, and boogie-woogie traditions of the southwest into what became known as Kansas City jazz. Preeminent among such outfits in the 1920s and early 1930s was the Alphonso Trent Orchestra headed by a piano player from Fort Smith (born in 1905) who took a Helena band called the Synco Six to Dallas where they changed their name, added four new members, and became a long-term smash at the Adolphus Hotel and radio station WFAA. Trent's orchestra toured widely, recorded several sessions for the Gennett label between 1928 and 1933, and became the "most professional, polished, and warmly remembered of all the bands in the Southwest."[15]

The list of prominent Arkansas jazz masters might start with Scott Joplin as the obvious headliner, but would mostly feature Little Rock musicians like Hayes Pillars and Snub Mosley, two members of Trent's band. Trombone player Mosley was born in Little Rock in 1905, while sax man Pillars, who went on to front the Jeter-Pillars Orchestra, was a North Little Rock native born in 1906. Vocalist Al Hibbler was a decade younger—born in 1915 (also in Little Rock), he starred with Jay McShann and Duke Ellington in the 1940s before recording his biggest hit, "Unchained Melody," in 1955. Tenor sax player "Pharaoh" Sanders came to fame in John Coltrane's sixties ensembles, but he too was born in Little Rock in 1940 and was backing R&B acts at local clubs as a high school student. But surely the first family of Little Rock's jazz scene would be the Porters. Pianist

Art Porter Sr.'s Arkansas roots run deep—born in Little Rock in 1934, he graduated from Dunbar High School in 1950 and from Arkansas AM&N (now the University of Arkansas at Pine Bluff) in 1954, taught at various Little Rock high schools and colleges, and performed widely (most famously with the Art Porter Trio) until his death in 1993. Art Porter Jr., born in 1961, started as a drummer in his father's trio, but ended up on saxophone. His was a rising star, with four albums to his credit, when he died in a 1996 boating accident in Thailand. Guitarist Eddie Fisher, another Little Rock native, was inducted into the Arkansas Jazz Hall of Fame in 2004.

But despite such early 1920s origins for widespread commercial recording of blues, country, and gospel music, Arkansas practitioners didn't manage to get recorded until 1927. Big Bill Broonzy was probably the first bluesman—he was recording in Chicago for Paramount in that year, although "Casey Bill" Weldon of Pine Bluff was also recorded as a member of the Memphis Jug Band in 1927. Some sources list Weldon as married to Memphis Minnie, the most popular female country blues performer of the period, but recent researchers have cast doubt on this story.[16] Brinkley native Louis Jordan made his first records for Brunswick in New York with the Jungle Band in 1929 but didn't hit it big until his own Tympany Five produced a remarkable run of jump blues and boogie hits in the late 1930s and 1940s. Jordan was born in 1908, learned clarinet from his music teacher father, and attended Arkansas Baptist College in Little Rock before going on the road in the 1920s for stints with both the Rabbit Foot Minstrels and the Ma Rainey Show on the southern TOBA circuit. (TOBA was officially

FIGURE 13 Alphonso Trent. *Courtesy of Arkansas History Commission, Little Rock*

FIGURE 14 Al Hibbler, Glenn
Miller, Count Basie. *Courtesy
of Old State House Museum
Collections, Little Rock*

the Theatre Owners' Booking Association, the primary agency for black
artists in the years between 1909 and the crash of 1929. The performers
themselves, overworked, housed miserably, and paid poorly, used to say
it really meant Tough On Black Asses.)

Another star of the 1930s was Peetie Wheatstraw, William Bunch to
his parents, who was born in Tennessee but grew up in Cotton Plant.
Wheatstraw was a genuinely flamboyant character who also billed himself as the "Devil's Son-in-law" and the "High Sheriff of Hell." He was

living in East St. Louis by 1929, and made his first records for Vocalion in Chicago in 1930. Wheatstraw played both guitar and piano and recorded more than 150 songs as a solo act and as an accompanist to such well-known artists as Lonnie Johnson and Kokomo Arnold before his career was cut short in a fatal car wreck in 1941. One index of his fame was the subsequent appearance of no fewer than three imitators—Peetie Wheatstraw's Brother (one Jimmy Gordon), Peetie Wheatstraw's Buddy, and Peetie's Boy.

Somewhat later to record was Robert Brown, Bill Broonzy's half-brother, who was better known as Washboard Sam. He was born in Walnut Ridge in 1910, worked with Memphis area bands in the early twenties, and was in Chicago by 1932 where beginning in 1935 he was frequently recorded as both a lead performer and accompanist for others on Bluebird, Vocalion, and other labels. Arbee Stidham, a harmonica player born in 1917 in De Valls Bluff, had formed the Southern Syncopators Band to play dances and clubs in and around Little Rock by the early 1930s. He also appeared on KARK radio in the same period, though he didn't record until the late 1940s. He was still

FIGURE 15 Louis Jordan. *Reproduced by permission of Getty Images*

recording in the 1970s. Another Arkansas bluesman who had a long and successful career was piano player Roosevelt "The Honeydripper" Sykes, who was born in Elmar in 1906 and began recording for OKeh in Chicago in 1929. Fifty years later he was still going strong, touring and recording in Europe in the 1960s and 1970s.

Jug band musician Dewey Corley was born in Halley in 1898, but he didn't record until 1934, as a member of the Memphis Jug Band, on the OKeh label. Charley Jordan was even older—he was born about 1890 in Mabelvale, but had settled in St. Louis where in the 1920s he worked with Roosevelt Sykes and Memphis Minnie and got shot in a bootlegging incident before making his first recordings for Vocalion in Chicago in 1930. Ernest Lawlars, known as "Little Son Joe," a guitar and washboard player from Hughes, also played extensively with Memphis Minnie, and unlike "Casey Bill" Weldon he seems in fact to have married her as well. He was born in 1900 and recorded briefly with Robert Wilkins in 1935 before his first sessions with Memphis Minnie in 1938. Floyd Jones, a guitar player born in 1917 in Marianna, wasn't recorded until the late 1940s. Fordyce native Guitar Pickett was recording in Houston in the 1940s and performing across a south Arkansas circuit centered in Camden and El Dorado.

The first Arkansas country music band to be recorded was a Searcy band called Pope's Arkansas Mountaineers, who went for a session with RCA Victor in Memphis on February 6, 1928. Though the personnel of the group varied, they were on that day a five-piece band featuring John Chism and his son Wallace on fiddle and guitar, brothers J. W. and "Tip" McKinney on banjo and vocals, plus guitarist John Sparrow. They recorded six songs, mostly traditional fiddle tunes, plus two "comic sermons" that were never released.

Just a few days later, on February 14, the Arkansas Barefoot Boys, a group from Vanndale who named themselves especially for the occasion, were also recorded in Memphis by the OKeh label. Featuring fiddle (Cyrus Futrell), guitar (Hubert Haines), and two harmonicas (James L. Sims and William Campbell), the group performed four tunes, of which two were released. One of these, "The Eighth of January," was among the state's most popular fiddle tunes. The Arkansas Barefoot Boys also recorded a comic number, "Benton County Hog Thief," featuring hog calls by fiddler Futrell, but like the "sermons" of Pope's Arkansas Mountaineers it was never released.

Several other Arkansas string bands managed to get recorded in 1928. A Hazen family band headed by Fiddlin' Bob Larkan cut two sessions in Memphis, one for OKeh in February and one for Vocalion in December, which resulted in a total of thirteen released tunes, while an outfit called the Reaves White County Ramblers—brothers Ike, Ira, and Lloyd Reaves plus Judsonia guitarist Fred Rumble—went all the way to Chicago for an April session that produced twelve tunes, all released on the Brunswick label. This group's output is especially interesting for two songs featuring the rarely recorded practice of "beating straws" (a second player striking the strings of the fiddle while the fiddler plays) and for the use of an organ accompaniment (by Lloyd Reaves) on every song.[17]

The largest and most durable Arkansas string band recorded in the 1920s was the flamboyantly named Dr. Smith's Champion Horse-Hair Pullers of Calico Rock. Organized and named by Izard County booster Dr. Henry Harlin Smith, who did not play, the band played several radio performances on KTHS in Hot Springs in 1926 but didn't record until a September 1928 Memphis date with Victor produced six numbers. The group for that session included four instrumentalists—Bryan Lackey and Clark Duncan on fiddle, Leeman Bone on guitar, and Ray Marshall on mandolin—plus a four-man vocal group (Graydon Bone, Roosevelt Garner, Odie Goatcher, and Hubert Simmons). The band continued to play locally until 1930 with varying personnel—at least thirteen musicians and singers were sometime members of the group.[18]

Another group to record after appearing on KTHS was Luke Hignight's Ozark Strutters, who recorded six instrumentals for Vocalion in Memphis on November 1928, including one called "Fort Smith Breakdown." Luke Hignite, born September 27, 1898, in the Arkansas Hollywood, in Clark County, played banjo and harmonica together; the Ozark Strutters were Frank Gardner on fiddle and Henry Tucker on guitar. Hignite was also recorded by OKeh in Memphis nine months earlier in February as a member of a three-piece band called Minton's Ozark String Band, but no songs from this session were released. Gardner played fiddle for this outfit too, while Sherman Tedder played guitar.

Two bands managed to be recorded more extensively than the other Arkansas groups—Ashley's Melody Men and George Edgin's Corn Dodgers. The former outfit was a Marshall string band centered on Hobart Ashley and his sons Gerald and Hugh, with Anson Fuller on fiddle and Homer Treat on banjo. Billing themselves on different occasions as the Hobart M. Ashley Singers, Ashley's Melody Makers, and Ashley's Melody Men, the group had three sessions with Victor in 1929, 1930, and 1932, the first two in Memphis and the third in Dallas. The group featured mostly original compositions by Hugh Ashley, who yodels as well as sings on his

"Somewhere in Arkansas" from the second session. Hugh Ashley also had a brief career as Elton Britt's predecessor in the Beverly Hill Billies before moving on to become a mayor of Harrison, Arkansas state representative, and music store operator.

George Edgin's Corn Dodgers were from Ozark, and included Delmar Hawkins and Earl Wright on guitar, Chesley Jones on mandolin, guitar, and harmonica, Brown Rich on bass fiddle, in addition to fiddler Edgin. Edgin's first session was a solo shot in November 1929 in Richmond, Indiana, for the Gennett label. For his second, for the same label in December, also in Richmond, he was accompanied by Hot Springs guitarist William Birkhead. No songs were released from either session.

In 1932 he was back for three more sessions, all with the Corn Dodgers, two in Richmond and the last in New York. Like Hugh Ashley, Edgin mixed his own tunes in with traditional material (including "Sally Goodin") and songs derived from other performers.

Only two other Arkansas bands were recorded as country music acts in the 1920s, and they cut very little material. The Morrison Twin Brothers String Band was headed by fiddlers Abbie and Apsie Morrison from Searcy County, who were accompanied on guitars by Abbie's sons Claude and Lawson when they recorded "Dry and Dusty" and "Ozark Waltz" in Memphis in 1930.[19] A. E. Ward and His Plowboys were from Walcott. Their brush with fame came in 1931, when they cut four tunes for Columbia in Atlanta. Ward, a fiddle player, was fifty-seven at the time, and the Plowboys were Ward's son Weisner and Bill Sawyer on guitar, plus Gene Morton on piano. Two songs were released, including "I'm Going to Leave Old Arkansas." The songs the early groups recorded show them as both up-to-date, familiar with popular radio and record tunes of the day, yet also well versed in the region's traditional repertoire. Thus George Edgin's Corn Dodgers recorded a version of "Dear Old Sunny South by the Sea" derived from Jimmie Rodgers and a very traditional "Sally Goodin'" for the same session, while the Arkansas Barefoot Boys combined "The Eighth of January" from the regional repertoire with a "Soldier's Joy" derived from a recording by Gid Tanner and the Skillet Lickers. For the people who played and sang them, the distinctions made by scholars between "folk" and "pop" songs were insignificant. For them the primary distinctions were entirely aesthetic; there was only music they and their neighbors enjoyed and music they didn't. They stuck with the former, and would have appreciated Bill Broonzy's alleged reply to an interviewer who asked if a given number was a folk song "I'd guess so," he reportedly said, "I never heard a mule sing it."

None of these 1920s bands enjoyed anything like sustained success in the record business, and with few exceptions they were relatively short-lived aggregations with constantly varying personnel who played primarily for local and area events. The musicians regarded themselves as semiprofessional at best, enjoying themselves, hoping for fame and fortune, but always depending upon other jobs to support themselves and their families. They got on the radio with ease, and on record with difficulty, and a few, like Madison County performers Bill and Toby Baker, succeeded in fully professional careers (they toured the vaudeville circuit with the Weaver Brothers and Elviry for three years at the end of the 1920s). But most performers in the first generation of Arkansas musicians to make records and appear on radio experienced little change in the basic shape of their lives. The trips to recording studios in distant cities were rare or unique events, and for the most part they continued to perform in their home communities for mostly local audiences. All this would soon change, however, with the arrival on the professional scene of a generation of musicians raised from the cradle on the new musical variety made available on records and radio.

But if Arkansas musicians were only rarely recorded in the industry's early years, the state itself was more often mentioned, and not always with the derision characteristic of the turn-of-the-century comic songs. One way to gauge the state's presence in blues recordings is to tally the references in the songs of Charley Patton and Robert Johnson. Patton's 1929 "Mississippi Boll Weevil Blues" includes Arkansas in the weevil's travel plans—"Let's leave Louisiana, we can go to Arkansas"—and "High Water Everywhere, Part II" of the same year describes flooding at Blytheville and "Marion City." The 1930 "Moon Going Down" makes reference to Helena—"I think I heard that Helena whistle blow."[20] Robert Johnson's "I Believe I'll Dust My Broom," recorded in his first session in 1936, also mentions Helena: "I'm gonna write a letter / telephone every town I know. / If I can't find her in West Helena / she must be in East Monroe, I know." Another formidable Arkansas woman (or perhaps the same one) is celebrated in the same session's "Terraplane Blues": "I've got a woman that I'm lovin' / way down in Arkansas." Things have turned bad in "32–20 Blues," the only song Johnson recorded at his second session (three days after the first). The song opens in threat: "If I send for my baby, / man and she don't come, / all the doctors in Hot Springs / sure can't help her none."[21]

Meanwhile several songs in the same vein pioneered by Eva Ware Barnett's "Arkansas" of 1916 continued to appear. James Braswell of Green Forest was directing a local Green Forest Cornet Band by 1892, but he saved his biggest splash for 1925 when he penned "In the Land of a Million Smiles," a number calculated to warm the hearts of every hotel keeper and restaurant owner in the region: "In taking your vacation," it opens, "I'll tell you where to go / Away down in the Ozarks, you'll love that place I know." Braswell, billed by supporters as "The Stephen Foster of the Ozarks," was a prolific writer, numbering among his compositions at least six "Ozark" titles (not including "Meet Me at the Basin in Eureka Springs").[22] Other examples from the period include A. M. Hutton's "Arkansas, the Wonder State," printed in Van Buren in 1928, John Breen's "I Want to Go Back to Arkansas," published in Chicago the same year, and Al Trace's "Little Sweetheart of the Ozarks," printed in 1937, also in Chicago. These songs offer mostly complimentary, idealized portraits of the state, but the old unflattering stereotypes that had previously produced "Down in the Arkansas" and "The Arkansas Boys" are still evident in pieces like Len Nash's "The Ozark Trail" and more especially Cole Porter's 1936 composition, "The Ozarks Are Callin' Me Home." Where the former song features a trigger-happy "old galoot" named Zeke, the latter presents a detailed portrait of sluttish women and men who beat them ("Paw givin' Maw her daily lickin'").

Other pieces of the period that did mention the state (or region) include the 1921 "Arkansas Blues" by Lucille Hegamin, Peetie Wheatstraw's "Hot Springs Blues," George Edgin's "My Ozark Mountain Home," Roosevelt Sykes's "Helena Blues," James White's "Way Down in Arkansaw," Will Ezell's "Arkansas Mill Blues," and "Where the Ozarks Kiss the Sky," co-written by Patsy Montana and Bob Miller. It wasn't a song about Arkansas, but composer Pinkey Tomlin of Eros had a big hit in 1934 with "The Object of My Affection."

Things got better for the state's country singers in the 1930s and 1940s. Patsy Montana and Elton Britt made it big, and harmonica virtuosos Lonnie Glosson and Wayne Raney played on the powerful "border radio" stations in Eagle Pass and Del Rio, Texas, as well as KARK in Little Rock. Glosson, a native of Judsonia, was the older man, and his playing on XEPN in 1934 so inspired Raney that he immediately hitchhiked to Eagle Pass to show off his own skills. He was thirteen. By 1938 the two were performing together, and Raney's biggest hit, the 1949 "Why Don't You Haul Off and Love Me," was co-written with Glosson. Raney, born in Wolf Bayou in 1921, also hosted his own show on Cincinnati station WCKY beginning in 1941, and in the late forties recorded several "hillbilly boogie" numbers with the Delmore Brothers that have recently been appreciated as predecessors of rockabilly. Raney died in 1993; Glosson in 2001. Claude Garner, another harmonica player with Arkansas roots, went from a Hot Springs gig with James Evans and the Dixie Mountaineers to touring with Eddy Arnold and appearances on the *Grand Ole Opry.*

FIGURE 16 Patsy Montana. *Courtesy of Old State House Museum Collections, Little Rock*

But it was the border stations, above all, that took the fame of Glosson and Raney far and wide. Raney, according to one source, sold a million harmonicas each year for five years running (he also sold harmonicas on his WCKY show). "Border radio did more for getting my name known than anything else," he said. Recalling that he usually followed the so-called Voice of Temperance, prohibitionist Sam Morris, he responded to Morris's

FIGURE 17 Wayne Raney *(at right). Courtesy of Old State House Museum Collections, Little Rock*

customary closing lines urging that alcoholic drinks "be taken down and poured in the river" by opening his own show with "Let's Gather at the River."[23] In 1957, trying (unsuccessfully) to catch the rockabilly wave, Raney cut "Shake Baby Shake." In such hitlust he was not alone— Bob Wills recorded "So Let's Rock" and country weeper George Jones, hiding under a "Thumper Jones" moniker, contributed a very forgettable "Rock It" to the trashpile.

Other Arkansas country singers who found success in the 1940s include David Myrick, better known as T. Texas Tyler and billed to the world as the Man with a Million Friends, and Lloyd and Floyd Armstrong, from De Witt, who as the five-year-old Armstrong Twins were appearing on Little Rock radio by 1935. Born in Mena in 1916, T. Texas Tyler settled in Los Angeles when he came out of the army in 1946 and was soon a success in several fields, appearing in the 1949 western *Horsemen of the Sierra* (1949) and hosting his own *Range Round Up* television show. In 1948 he hit it big with two songs, "Dad Gave My Dog Away" and "Deck of Cards," the latter an ancient "recitation" number featuring a soldier's use of playing cards as a mnemonic device for Christian devotions. The ace reminds us of the one and only God, the deuce the Bible's division into Old and New Testament, the trey the Holy Trinity. And so on. This piece has been a big earner for decades, combining piety and patriotism as few others have managed— Red Sovine's "The Viet Nam Deck of Cards," Red River Dave's Korean War era "Red Deck of Cards," Cowboy Copas's "Cowboy's Deck of Cards," and Wink Martindale's later hit with the same title as Tyler's (1959) are among the more notable renditions.

The Wilburn Brothers (Doyle and Teddy) were from Hardy, and started as a family group, singing on street corners and broadcasting on Jonesboro's WBTM in the late 1930s. A brief stint on the *Grand Ole Opry* in 1940 was ended by child labor laws. Following U.S. Army service in Korea, the Wilburns returned to the *Opry* as a duo, toured with Webb Pierce and Faron Young, and scored several mid-level hits ("I Wanna Wanna Wanna" (1956) and "Trouble's Back in Town" (1962) may be the best known). Busy in many areas of the country music business, the Wilburns also operated a management/booking agency (their star client was Loretta Lynn) and hosted their own 1960s television show.

Even bigger than the Wilburns or Tyler was Mineola's Jimmy Wakely, born in 1914, who got his big break in 1940 when Gene Autry hired him away from an Oklahoma City radio show to appear on his Hollywood *Melody Ranch* program. By 1944 he was a singing cowboy movie star himself, and in 1948 he took two songs—"I Love You So Much It Hurts" and "One Has My Name, the Other Has My Heart"—to the top spot on country charts. Movies, songs, even comic books—Wakely in the late 1940s and early 1950s was a major star. The "Slipping Around" he did as a duet with Margaret Whiting was big enough to merit a follow-up "I'll Never Slip Around Again," and the same duo also hit it big with "A Bushel and a Peck." Dale Evans was born in Texas, but she went to high school in Osceola before heading west for a long career as a movie and television cowgirl with Roy Rogers (her husband since 1947).

FIGURE 18 The Wilburn Brothers, Teddy *(left)* and Doyle. *Courtesy of Old State House Museum Collections, Little Rock*

There was also an active country music scene in the state's northern and northeastern sections. Ask old-timers in Searcy, Newport, Jonesboro, or Heber Springs and you'll hear stories of bands like the Sunny Slope Boys (Hal and Johnny Scroggins, Glynn Hipp, Jerry Stevens, W. T. Bittle), shows like *Clark's Brand-Nu Opry* in Heber Springs, and radio stations like Searcy's KWCB.

Religious music had been included on even the earliest commercial recordings. The venerable gospel standard "Blessed Assurance," for example, written by the prolific blind composer Fanny Crosby (with

FIGURE 19 Cowboy movie star Jimmy Wakely *(at center, in fancy shirt). Courtesy of Old State House Museum Collections, Little Rock*

music by Phoebe Palmer Knapp) in 1873, was on record by 1900, and the Dinwiddie Colored Quartet was recording spirituals by 1902. Black and white gospel traditions, even as each developed its own distinctive performance styles, have shared repertoires from the beginning. Thus "Blessed Assurance" was soon recorded by black singers—Texas shouter Madame Emily Bram's 1951 rendition is a strong contender for the most powerful vocal ever recorded—just as "Go Wash in the Beautiful Pool," written by pioneer black gospel composer Charles Albert Tindley and first published in 1901, had been adopted by southern white singers by the late 1920s. Ollie Gilbert sang it in Mountain View in the 1960s for a record album with notes by Jimmy Driftwood.[24] An especially vivid instance of such interactions occurs with "Old Time Religion," a song that first appears in white tradition in 1891, when Charles Davis Tillman published it (with copyright) in a revival songbook. But the song clearly derives from the spiritual tradition popularized by touring choirs from black colleges in the 1870s, and it was in fact included in an 1880 publication, *The Story of the Jubilee Singers and Their Songs,* by J. B. Marsh. Early recordings of the song include versions by the white Haydn Quartet (1910), the black Tuskegee Institute Singers (1916), plus a 1910 Edison cylinder recording by Polk Miller and His Old South Quartet. The Old South Quartet was black, while Miller was a white Civil War veteran.

But despite these early appearances of religious music on record, the primary emphasis in the early years of gospel music was on the production and distribution of printed songbooks rather than recordings. In black sacred music this may derive from songbooks associated with the touring Fisk University Jubilee Singers (Theodore F. Seward's *Jubilee Songs,* published in 1872) and the Hampton Singers (Thomas P. Fenner's *Cabin and Plantation Songs,* issued in 1874). Gospel pioneers Charles A. Tindley, Lucie Eddie Campbell, and Thomas A. Dorsey also emphasized the distribution of songs by way of printed music marketed at annual meetings of the National Baptist Convention.[25]

In white tradition a similar emphasis may owe most to the huge influence of Ira Sankey's *Sacred Songs and Solos* collections, first compiled to support his evangelistic work with Dwight L. Moody in the 1870s. Gospel publishing in the south also stressed the sale of printed songbooks, and was dominated first by the Vaughan Company of Lawrenceburg, Tennessee,

FIGURE 20 Singing School at Philadelphia, Columbia County, July 30, 1914. *Courtesy of Southwest Arkansas Regional Archives, Washington, Arkansas*

which published its first songbook, *Gospel Chimes,* in 1900, and later by the Stamps-Baxter Company in Dallas, founded in 1926. The latter company maintained an Arkansas branch at Pangburn, mostly in the person of Luther G. Presley, a native of Faulkner County (born in 1887) who in a lifetime of composing published more than one thousand songs and worked in the songbook business with at least three houses. Described in one Stamps-Baxter publication as "liberal in his views, consistent in his practice, consecrated in service," Presley is best remembered today for "I'd Rather Have Jesus."[26]

Other Arkansas gospel pioneers were E. M. Bartlett, who established the Hartford Music Company and the associated Hartford Music Institute, and Floyd E. Hunter, who combined timber and oil-field work with gospel songwriting and singing school teaching. Hunter was born

in 1903, and raised in various small communities in eastern Arkansas (Glenwood, Center Point, Cauthron, Crystal Springs). In 1926 he moved to Hot Springs, where he sang on KTHS, published his first songs in Hartford songbooks, and taught more than one hundred singing schools. In 1939 he became president of a very active Arkansas State Quartet Convention, and in 1945 he went to work for Stamps-Baxter. He was no Luther Presley, but Hunter did turn out some 130 songs, of which the best known is probably "Way Down Deep in My Soul." Other Arkansas gospel publishers included the Central Music Company of Little Rock, the Jeffress Music Company of Crossett, and the Eureka Music Company of Siloam Springs.

FIGURE 21 Fiddlin' Jake and George Baize, Ozark Folk Festival, Eureka Springs, 1952. *Courtesy of Special Collections Division, University of Arkansas Libraries, Fayetteville*

The main business of all these enterprises was the publication and sale of songbooks, but many maintained music institutes and sponsored touring quartets as well. The Hartford Company, like Vaughan and Stamps-Baxter, published a magazine (*The Herald*) that "kept fans up on the latest singing conventions, songbooks, and the whereabouts of various company-sponsored quartets and groups."[27] The well-known gospel composer Albert E. Brumley, born in Oklahoma in 1905, studied in Hartford from 1926 to 1930, sang bass with the Hartford Quartet, and later went on to write "I'll Fly Away," "Jesus, Hold My Hand," "If We Never Meet Again," and some six hundred other sacred songs. He was especially proud of the fact that "If We Never Meet Again" was Elvis Presley's mother's favorite song and that several condemned killers reportedly went to their deaths consoled by the singing of Brumley tunes. Brumley is so revered in Arkansas today that the state's largest gospel meeting, a three-day affair held every August since 1969, is called the Albert E. Brumley Sundown to Sunup Gospel Sing.[28]

Arkansas gospel singers were also late getting recorded. Sister Rosetta Tharpe opened her career with a song called "Rock Me" in 1938. Despite the title, it wasn't rock and roll. It's an up-tempo song, but what's rocking is a cradle. Roberta Martin had moved to Illinois long before she became famous with the Roberta Martin singers, but she was born Roberta Winston in Helena in 1907. Madame Ernestine B. Washington first recorded in the forties, though by then, Arkansas roots in the background, she was in Brooklyn, married to Bishop F. D. Washington of the Temple Church of God in Christ, and billed as the "Songbird of the East." At least two Arkansas performers worked both sides of the blues/gospel fence, beginning in gospel in the 1920s and 1930s and moving into blues in the 1960s. Bonnie Jefferson, from Shoal Creek, and Vance Powell, from Warren, both worked first in gospel groups, the former touring Arkansas with a family group, and the latter singing with the Evening Melody Boys and other groups in the St. Louis area.

The best-known Arkansas figure in white gospel from this period is remembered now as an Ohio television evangelist, but Rex Humbard got his start in Hot Springs, performing with a family group on the KTHS "Saturday Night Jamboree" before moving to Dallas in 1939 and later organizing the well-known Cathedrals group for his Cathedral of

FIGURE 22 Rosetta Tharpe. *Reproduced by permission of Getty Images*

Tomorrow in 1963. Humbard was born in Little Rock in 1919, to parents who met at a preaching convention in Eureka Springs.[29]

Scholars and students of traditional music were also quick to take advantage of the new recording technologies. In 1936 both John Lomax and Sidney Robertson Cowell visited Mena to record Emma Dusenbury. Vance Randolph had been earlier—six songs from *Ozark Folksongs* are credited to her singing on September 4, 1930—and in 1938 she would be visited several times by a young man named Lee Hays, then a student at nearby Commonwealth College, the "radical school" soon to be hounded out of existence by the forces of virulent decency. More would be heard from him later. In 1936 the Library of Congress also recorded versions of "The Girls Won't Do to Trust" and "Down in Arkansas" from Gilbert Fike in Little Rock; in 1939 Lomax recorded Irvin Lowry singing "Joe the Grinder" at the Cummins prison in Gould; Alan Lomax, Lewis Jones, and John W. Work recorded William Brown and Willie Blackwell at Sadie Beck's Plantation in Crittenden County in 1942, and Vance Randolph recorded Irene Carlisle singing "The Brazos River" in Farmington the same year.[30] Batesville native John Quincy Wolf, a professor at Southwestern University in Memphis, began his recording of Ozark singers in the 1940s, and Randolph's great regional collection, *Ozark Folksongs,* a huge four-volume work featuring songs contributed by scores of Arkansas and Missouri singers, began appearing in 1946.

By 1940, too, Lee Hays, the kid from Commonwealth College who had listened to Emma Dusenbury, had gone to New York determined to put music to work. Hays was the son of an Arkansas Methodist preacher, William Hays, who died in an auto accident in 1927 while the family was living in Booneville. Lee, born in Little Rock in 1914, was thirteen. By 1934 he had come under the influence of a firebrand radical Presbyterian preacher named Claude Williams, who until he was fired pastored a church in the Arkansas Paris, in Logan County, and committed himself to the life of political activism that took him first to Commonwealth and Emma Dusenbury and then to New York and the Almanac Singers. The Almanacs, formed in 1940, featured Hays, Harvard-boy-turned-proletarian Pete Seeger, and West Virginia University graduate Millard Lampell as original members. Peter Hawes was added to the group later, and Woody Guthrie joined in 1941. The Almanac Singers toured the country performing for union organizations, folk music fans, and college students, and also made several records before disbanding during World War II. In 1948, with the war over, Seeger and Hays joined again, this time with Fred Hellerman and Ronnie Gilbert, to form the Weavers, a short-lived though very popular group who took their name if little political attitude from Gerhart

Hauptmann's angry 1891 play about a Silesian workers' revolt in 1844. A "folk revival" was just around the corner.[31]

But surely the single most-significant recording made in the 1930s in Arkansas starred not aspiring musicians in search of fame and fortune but black convicts from a prison work gang singing for Library of Congress researcher John Lomax and his driver and assistant Huddie Ledbetter at the end of September and beginning of October, 1934. The song was a wonderful piece, new to both Lomax and Ledbetter, the story of a tall-tale train so fast it "left Memphis at half past nine" and "made it back to Little Rock at eight forty-nine."[32] That was, the men sang, a "mighty good road," a train for brave riders only: "If you want to ride it you got to ride it like you're flyin'."[33] It was the voices of bound men raised in celebration of freedom, prisoners who could go nowhere exhilarated by imagining movement so fast it was flight.

It was, of course, "The Rock Island Line," and Lomax and Ledbetter heard it twice in their week's work in Arkansas, first in Little Rock, where they also recorded street musicians George Ryan and "Blind Pete," and later at the Cummins prison farm in Gould. The singers on the first recording are not named, but the Cummins group was headed by a singer from Camden named Kelly Pace. In 1947, writing his autobiography, Lomax still remembered the scene:

> Down the road and around the bend ran at top speed a group of laughing, shouting convicts with the guard loping behind, a shotgun braced against his saddle and pointing straight up. At last these exulting boys were to "git on dat machine." They came up panting from their wild race. Soon a picked group gathered about the microphone and sang a wonderful cotton-picking song, a song about a Southwestern railroad, the rhythm of which fits into the movements of swift hands grabbing the white locks from the bolls of cotton and stuffing handfuls into their dragging sacks. Eight to sing, one to whistle like a locomotive. They picked that cotton so fast they seemed to feel as if they were on an express train tearing through the cotton patch on the famous Rock Island line.[34]

Ledbetter, just out of prison himself at the time (Lomax had first encountered him in 1933 at the Louisiana state prison at Angola), would make the song and himself famous, recording it many times, beginning in 1937. Billed as Leadbelly, a name he'd picked up in the Texas Sugarland prison back in the 1920s, he performed the song so regularly that, like "Goodnight Irene" and "The Midnight Special," it is today remembered first of all as his song. But Leadbelly didn't create "The Rock Island Line." He heard it in two Arkansas prisons in 1934. What he did was take it to the world.

But long before there were records by Broonzy, Tharpe, or Pope's Arkansas Mountaineers, Arkansas listeners were buying Jimmie Rodgers and Blind Lemon Jefferson hits and playing them on their newly purchased phonographs. On their radios they were listening to everything from barn dances and fiddlers and jazz bands to church choirs and college glee clubs and western swing outfits. Literally hundreds of local and national music shows were on the air; the hills, the Gulf coastal plain, and the Mississippi Delta were alive with the sound of Arkansas music.

It was a cultural explosion of then-unprecedented impact—the lid was simply lifted from what had been a largely local world, and suddenly people in Arkansas were hearing not only the music of other people from faraway places, but also the music of places geographically near but heretofore socially and culturally quite distinct. The whole globe, as a famous academic and an Arkansas rock band would put it nearly half a century later, was becoming a village. Electricity had come to Arkansas.

FIGURE 23 Sister Rosetta Tharpe's guitar. *Courtesy of Old State House Museum Collections, Little Rock*

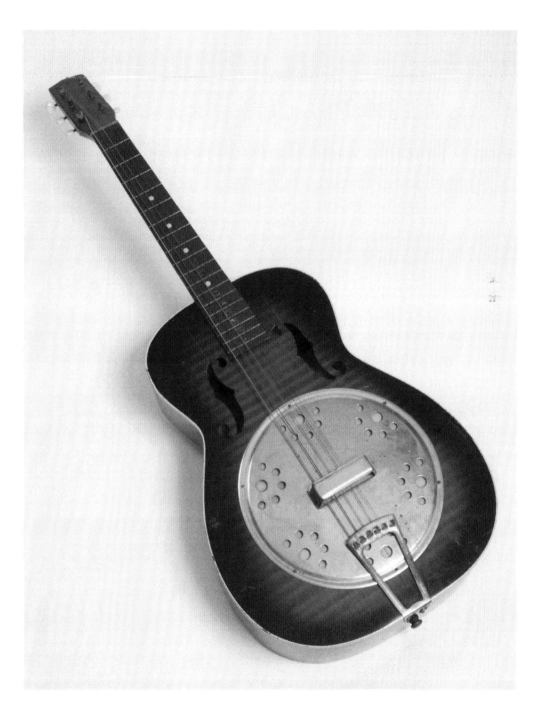

3 ✿ A MIXTURE RICH AND STRANGE

At some time in the decade after the end of World War II rock and roll came to Arkansas. In retrospect it may appear an inevitable consequence of the wholesale meeting and intermixture of musical traditions following the widespread introduction of radio and phonograph records into local life, but at the time it seemed to many a phenomenon unimaginably strange. Most called its earliest appearances rockabilly, and of all the subsequent attempts at matching recollection to the lived experience, perhaps Nick Tosches's try comes closest, successful because of its excesses, like the music itself: "What made rockabilly such a drastically new music was its spirit, a thing that bordered on mania . . . Country music in recent years had not known such vehement emotion, nor had black music. Rockabilly was the face of Dionysos, full of febrile sexuality and senselessness; it flushed the faces of new housewives and made pink teenage boys reinvent themselves as flaming creatures."[1]

Some have located the change early. Rockabilly baritone Sleepy LaBeef, born in Smackover, July 20, 1935, says it happened when Rosetta Tharpe recorded "Strange Things Happening Every Day" in 1944. Others lay praise (or blame) on the "jump" blues of Brinkley native Louis Jordan's Tympany Five or on the "hillbilly boogie" of the Delmore Brothers, featuring the harmonica wizardry of Wayne Raney. Not even gospel music was exempt— the Delmore Brothers' 1945 hit, "Hillbilly Boogie" was followed in 1948 by a "Gospel Boogie" first recorded by the Homeland Harmony Quartet. Despite attacks from offended listeners for whom the association of gospel and boogie was an abomination, the record did well (and did even better when Pat Boone recorded it a decade later as "Wonderful Time Up There"). It was soon recorded by other artists, black and white (including Rosetta Tharpe). Not only did the church, in the persons of Sam Cooke, Little Richard, Johnny Cash, and Jerry Lee Lewis (expelled from Waxahachie Bible College for adding barrelhouse riffs to chapel hymns), march flamboyantly out to rock the world, the world in turn rocked right back into

FIGURE 24 Louis Jordan's saxophone. *Courtesy of Old State House Museum Collections, Little Rock*

the church, especially into its more Pentecostal congregations. Gospel, and rock, have never been the same.

Purists among rock historians have meanwhile insisted on more local origins—perhaps the public appearances of the "King Biscuit Time" stars in delta towns in the 1940s, or the shows in September 1954, when Bill Black, Scotty Moore, and Elvis Presley pushed their first Sun release with club dates in Helena or Forrest City. Levon Helm, future Hawk for Ronnie Hawkins and Band drummer, was then a reluctant schoolboy in Marvell. He witnessed both acts firsthand, and was twice mightily impressed: Sonny Boy Williamson "overpowered you with his amplified open-air country R&B," Peck Curtis was "a hell of a drummer," and Elvis at Helena's Catholic Club "in his pink jacket and jet-black hair" had the place in pandemonium. "The kids around us were screaming so loud it was hard to focus on what the musicians were doing; all I remember is they were rockin' *down*. It was hot. It was crackin'."[2] When Presley brought this show to Little Rock's Robinson Auditorium on May 16, 1956 (not his first appearance), he was headed for national stardom, but still sufficiently new for the local DJ to introduce his first number as "Heartbreak Motel."

Or perhaps the shift occurred more subtly, in several places at many times, including the moment when Fayetteville jazzman Buddy Hayes introduced young Ronnie Hawkins to Howlin' Wolf and took him to Fort Smith to hear musicians like "Gatemouth" Brown, and the day KFFA added Muddy Waters's "Hoochie Coochie Man" or "I Got My Mojo Working" to its playlist.

But the change itself, not its debatable date, is what matters. Sam Phillips long ago become

FIGURE 25 Frank Frost's harmonica. *Courtesy of Old State House Museum Collections, Little Rock*

famous as the man who set out to find "a white man who had the Negro sound and the Negro feel," knowing in his bones that success in such a search would bring him "a billion dollars." He's famous because with Elvis Presley, Jerry Lee Lewis, and a host of lesser redneck lights he succeeded beyond his or their wildest imaginings. But in fact things were much more complicated. Despite the obvious presence of blues and R&B in both its repertoire and its performance styles, rockabilly music was white at its heart, "full of the redneck ethos."[3]

More important, Phillips didn't set out to find white singers at all; his explicit purpose was to record black music from black singers. And he did it, too. The Memphis Recording Service opened its doors in 1950; Elvis Presley's first record was made in 1954. From the recordings he made in 1951 for sale or lease to other labels, through the early releases on his own Sun label from 1952 to 1954, the emphasis on black music is overwhelming. His recordings for Chess in Chicago and Modern in Los Angeles put such artists as B. B. King, Howlin' Wolf, and Ike Turner on record at the beginning of their careers. Phillips always rated Chester Burnett, aka Howlin' Wolf, as his greatest find, even over Presley and Lewis. He first heard him on a fifteen-minute Hadacol show over KWEM in West Memphis. Of the first thirty-five records Phillips made at Sun—Presley's first record was the thirty-sixth (if one includes an unreleased first effort by Walter Horton and Jack Kelly)—two-thirds are by black blues and R&B artists. Most went nowhere, like the 1952 second issue, "Dreary Nights" and "Nuthin' But the Blues" by Forrest City disc jockey Walter Bradford and the Big City Four, but James Cotton, Little Junior Parker, Little Milton, Walter Horton, and Rufus Thomas all went on to substantial careers.

Herman "Little Junior" Parker was a Mississippi native who learned harmonica from Sonny Boy Williamson in West Memphis and soon had his own show on KWEM. He's best known today for his 1953 "Mystery Train," covered by Presley in 1955. James Cotton was a West Memphis harmonica player who played on some of Phillips's recordings of Howlin' Wolf before cutting his first Sun release in 1954. At his second Sun session (which produced "Cotton Crop Blues") Cotton was accompanied by the spectacular Cherry Valley guitarist Auburn "Pat" Hare, "the most aggressive picker to work at Phillips' studio." At the same session Hare recorded his own "I'm Gonna Murder My Baby," a "chilling performance of unparalleled menace" in which the singer addressed the judge prior to committing the crime. Phillips had the good sense to withhold this number, but twenty years later it was issued on a Dutch bootleg, and was later released on a Sun anthology in the United States. Hare went on to play with Junior Parker in Houston and after that with Cotton and Otis Spann in Muddy Waters's band in Chicago, but his career ended abruptly in 1962 when he did indeed murder his baby in Minneapolis and was shipped to the state slam in Stillwater, where he ended his days in 1980.[4]

Another early rock and roller (though he was really an R&B crooner) who ended his life under lock and key was Little Willie John. Born in Cullendale (or Mabelvale, pick your source) in 1937, John's biggest hit was the 1956 "Fever," covered by both Elvis Presley and Peggy Lee. He also produced a marvelously pathetic "Need Your love So Bad" and other minor hits (his "Leave My Kitten Alone" was covered by the Beatles) before a manslaughter conviction for a Seattle stabbing sent him up for 8–20 at Walla Walla State Penitentiary in 1966. John died in 1968; he was inducted into the Rock and Roll Hall of Fame in 1996.

Later on things changed at Sun, with the advent of Phillips's amazing collection of "hillbilly cats" from all over the south and southwest—"All of 'em were totally nuts," said record industry publicist Bill Williams. "I think every one of them must have come in on the midnight train from nowhere. I mean, it was like they came from outer space." With Phillips's help they made a new music, and took it to new places, and smashed a hundred social norms in the process. But the original emphasis on black artists, on blues and R&B styles, remains decisive. "I went out into this no-man's land," said the man himself, "and I knocked the shit out of the color line."[5]

One of the first country music singers to record at Sun was Howard Seratt, a gospel singer from Manila who cut "Troublesome Waters" and "I Must Be Saved" in late 1953 or early 1954. Phillips loved him—"I never heard a person, no matter what category of music, could sing as beautifully" —but Seratt refused to perform secular material, and Phillips never recorded him again. Sun was also home to Sonny Burgess, born in Newport in 1931, whose 1956 release, "We Wanna Boogie," backed with "Red-

Headed Woman" has been described as "among the rawest recordings released during the first flowering of rock 'n' roll." Two other candidates for such a title would surely be "Flying Saucer Rock and Roll" and "Red Hot," 1957 releases by Billy Riley and His Little Green Men. Both songs, as somebody once said of Little Richard's approach to singing, hit the ground sprinting and accelerated. Jerry Lee Lewis pounded piano on the first cut, and Brookings native Roland Janes provided guitar for Riley's screaming vocals on both, but despite their energy neither record was a hit and the Pocahontas native soon left Sun a bitter rocker, convinced that Phillips was neglecting his career to promote Lewis. Riley is still going strong—he wowed a college crowd at a 1996 Fayetteville concert with a blues-dominated acoustic set. And Sun historians, surveying the whole output of the groundbreaking label, have given Riley and his band high marks: "Win, lose, or draw, Riley always had one of the hottest working bands in the mid-South."[6] Another early rockabilly with a still-remembered wildman stage act was Jonesboro's Bobby Lee Trammell, who rose (or fell) from the stage to the Arkansas House of Representatives. Walter Bittle, who grew up near Heber Springs, also started as a rocker, playing the Oasis, the Wagon Wheel, and other Highway 67 clubs with his brother Loy and Glynn Hipp, but ended up in gospel instead of politics. Bill Gaither and the Goodman Family recorded his "I Hold a Clear Title to the Mansion."

A major star with as good a claim as any to the title of Arkansas's premier pioneer rock and roller is Conway Twitty, who was tearing up clubs and roadhouses as Harold Jenkins and the Rockhousers long before he hit it big as a country star in the late 1960s. It was Jenkins, too, at the time just reborn as Conway Twitty, who first blazed the trail to Canada for Billy Riley and especially Ronnie Hawkins to follow. (The name change was suggested by a talent manager named Don Seat, but the inspired choice was made by Jenkins himself, with help from a road map. He combined two town names—Conway, Arkansas, and Twitty, Texas, just as Marion Slaughter had done more than thirty years earlier to become Vernon Dalhart. In fact his closest connection with Conway came in 1960 when he hired drummer Tommy "Pork Chop" Markham, a native of that city and member of the local Aristocrats band, to replace Jack Nance in his road band.)

Born the son of a riverboat pilot in 1933 in Friar's Point, Mississippi, and raised mostly in Helena, Jenkins made his debut on KFFA at twelve, singing Ernest Tubb's hit "Our Baby's Book" on a show featuring a local string band called the Arkansas Cotton Choppers. Two or three years later he was a regular himself, performing on Saturday mornings with two school friends as the Phillips County Ramblers. In 1956, just out of the army, Jenkins recorded eight songs for Sam Phillips at Sun. None was released, though "Rockhouse" was later brought out by Roy Orbison. In 1957 he cut three losers for Mercury, claimed his new name, and headed for Canada. They started out in Hamilton, Ontario (at the Flamingo Lounge), where first responses ranging from incredulity to outright hostility eventually gave way to a fanatically loyal fan base. Soon they moved up to the Ontario London (at the Brass Rail), and finally to Toronto's Brown Derby, where they were still working when "It's Only Make Believe" (on MGM) went to #1 in 1958.

Sensing the end of the rockabilly ride, Twitty made himself over as a country artist in 1965, and by 1968 he'd made it to the top again (with "Next in Line"). Working solo and in duets with Loretta Lynn, he produced hit after hit in the seventies and eighties. He was soon known as much for his varied business ventures as for his music—Twitty Enterprises over the years brought out Twitty burgers, Conway the Twitty Bird (who sang with the star on a *Merry Twismas* album), Conway Twitty Mobile Homes (Twailers was *not* its name, contrary to rumor), the Nashville Sounds minor league baseball team, and above all Twitty City, a "multimillion- dollar tourist complex" in Hendersonville, Tennessee. By 1975 Twitty went international, recording "Privet Radost," a Russian version of "Hello Darlin'." The American commander presented it to his Russian counterpart during a joint Russian-American space venture.[7]

Another 1975 story (from July 5) is local and international at the same time, a dark comedy featuring Rolling Stones Keith Richards and Ron Wood in starring roles. The Stones had just played Memphis (on July 4) and were due next in Dallas (on July 6). Arkansas had no slot—until Richards decided that a not-to-be-missed opportunity to experience the Natural State had presented itself. Major adventures followed, centered on their rented limo getting pulled over in Fordyce. Before it was over there was a mysterious hitchhiker, charges of cocaine and concealed weapon possession, Dallas TV crews on the scene, and charter planes on the Fordyce runway. Richards eventually posted bail of $162.75, charges were dropped, the judge posed for photos with the Stones, and Richards's dagger (the concealed weapon) was soon displayed on the courtroom wall.[8]

From its rockabilly and R&B beginnings, rock and roll sped off in many directions, with Arkansas musicians along on every ride. The 1960s saw a lively music scene with a host of bands inspired by "British invasion" sounds and (a bit later) the Stax-Volt soul hits out of Memphis. Little Rock had the best-known regional bands—the Coachmen, the Romans, Dutch Masters—but the Egyptians, another once-popular outfit, came out of Hot Springs. These bands put out 45s on Earl Fox's My label, and some of them got good regional distribution and decent hearings on local radio stations. (In 1999 the Butler Center for Arkansas Studies assembled a twenty-five-track CD, *The Little Rock Sound: 1965–1969,* with a nice selection of this music with good notes by Bill Jones. The tracks by the Culls hold up unusually well.) Meanwhile, North Little Rock guitarist Louie Shelton, who got a young start playing in Little Rock's *Barnyard Frolic* show with Shelby Cooper and the Dixie Mountaineers before he was in his teens, had already followed Glen Campbell to California, where his session work included the Monkees' "Last Train to Clarksville" and the young Michael Jackson's first Jackson 5 hit, "I Want You Back."

Nearly a decade earlier, in March of 1957, Little Rock's KTHV premiered a rock and roll dance program, *Steve's Show,* beating *American Bandstand*'s national appearance by almost six months. Hosted by flamboyant DJ, weatherman, and soon-to-be congressional aide and investment banker Steve Stephens, *Steve's Show* was soon the biggest thing going with area teenagers, operating on a six-day-per-week format and drawing dancers from all over central Arkansas. White dancers. The show, born in the years wracked by school desegregation turmoil, was wholly segregated—though one member of the "Steve's Show Dancers" troupe recalled occasions when the walls came down on the dance floors too:

> I recall one time being at Robinson Auditorium, for one of their rock & roll extravaganzas with lots of fabulous entertainers, such as The Imperials, Bo Diddley, Chuck Berry, Ike and Tina Turner, etc. I don't remember if we danced on stage upstairs, it might have been in the aisles, but the real fun came when we went downstairs for the "black show," which was held in the basement of Robinson.

In those days, African Americans couldn't come to the white show, so the performers would put on another show later, and it was always better. We danced on a stage downstairs.[9]

Alongside all this rocking and rolling, "King Biscuit Time" was still going strong down in Helena. Robert Lockwood had moved north to Chicago in 1950 and later Cleveland (in 1960), and Sonny Boy Williamson was gone a good bit of the time, though he returned regularly, especially in the last year of his life. In fact his death was only discovered when he failed to show up for the show on May 25, 1965. But Peck Curtis was still drumming on the show in the 1960s, and by that time a younger generation of bluesmen had arrived to take over the other instruments. One was Frank Frost, born in Augusta in 1936, who learned harmonica from Sonny Boy Williamson himself, mastered guitar and piano as well, and was appearing on KFFA by the early 1960s. In 1962, working with (who else?) Sam Phillips, he recorded "some of the last truly great blues recordings to emerge from Memphis."[10] (The "great" may stand unchallenged, but British blues fans should be wary of judging the vital signs of American traditions—Broonzy was billing himself to Yankees and Europeans as "the last blues singer alive" in the 1940s.) In 1996, three years before his death in 1999, Frost headlined a live broadcast of the revived "King Biscuit Show" from the Old State House Museum.

Yet another Arkansas harmonica player to achieve some fame was Hughes native Joe Bennie Pugh, known as Forrest City Joe, who didn't play "King Biscuit Time" but did work with Williamson and Howlin' Wolf on the KWEM Hadacol show, and cut an album for Atlantic in 1959. And even this doesn't exhaust the state's list of harmonica stars. Junior Wells, a major harp player on the Chicago club scene in the 1960s, was born in Tennessee but raised in West Memphis and Marion, and James Harris (from Earle), Elmon "Drifting Slim" Mickle (from Keo), Earlee Payton (from Pine Bluff), Mack Simmons (from Twist), George "Harmonica" Smith (from Helena) all enjoyed success as professional musicians. Down in the southwestern section of the state a hot band in the 1950s was Jay Franks's Rockets of Rhythm, a ten-piece R&B outfit. Ashdown and Texarkana area guitarist Nelson Carson and piano player Trenton Cooper, who was born in Hope, both played with Franks's band before appearing on a 1983 collection of Arkansas blues entitled *Keep It to Yourself.*

Arkansas's northeastern corner produced its own star in many-named saxophone player Jr. Walker (a k a Audrey DeWalt and Oscar G. Mixon). Born in Blytheville sometime between 1931 and 1942 (his dates vary as much as his names), Walker had his biggest hit with the 1965 "Shotgun," but as Jr. Walker and the All-Stars he was a Motown regular from the sixties through the eighties. Walker died in 1995.

Jimmy Witherspoon played bass, not harmonica, but he also enjoyed a long and successful career. Born in Gurdon in 1923, he began singing in church as a child, but turned professional after World War II, working mostly with the Jay McShann Band in California in the late 1940s and with many other groups thereafter. Witherspoon toured Europe in 1961 with the Buck Clayton All Stars, Japan in 1963 with Count Basie, and by the mid-1970s had played everything from Johnny Carson's *Tonight Show* to the Montreux Music Festival in Switzerland.

FIGURE 26 Frank Frost. *Courtesy of Leslie R. Chin*

Larry "Totsy" Davis, born in Missouri but raised in Little Rock, the Arkansas England, in Lonoke County, and Pine Bluff, was another successful Arkansas bluesman. Like several other prominent bluesmen (Earl Hooker, Son Seals) Davis started as a drummer but later concentrated on guitar. Sometime around 1951 he sat in with B. B. King at Little Rock's Club Morocco, and after touring in the mid-1950s with the Bill Fort and Hugh Holloway bands he made his first recordings for the Houston-based Duke label in 1958. Davis, who died in 1994, is best remembered for "Texas Flood," which he wrote and recorded in Houston twenty years before it was a hit for Stevie Ray Vaughan. He enjoyed his greatest success at the end of his career, when his *Sooner or Later* CD was released to wide acclaim in 1992. Mississippi-born Fenton Robinson got his start playing with Davis (he handles the guitar solo on the original version of "Texas Flood"), and lived in Little Rock while working regularly with Davis in the 1950s. Robinson moved to Chicago in the 1960s and recorded several widely acclaimed albums (most notably *Somebody Loan Me a Dime* in 1975) on Bruce Iglauer's Alligator label. Robinson died in 1997.

Even more widely known than Davis or Robinson was Luther Allison, who was born in Mayflower in 1939, and lived in Forrest City as a child. In 1969, after contributing two cuts to the *Sweet Home Chicago* anthology on Chicago's Delmark label, Allison recorded his first solo effort, *Love Me Mama* (also on Delmark). European concert tours generated such enthusiastic responses that by 1980 Allison had more or less permanently relocated to Paris. In 1994, however, Allison launched an American comeback, signing with Chicago's Alligator label and putting out three albums in four years—*Soul Fixin' Man* (1994), *Blue Streak* (1995), and *Reckless* (1997). Prizes fell down like rain—multiple W. C. Handy Awards, two Blues Entertainer of the Year citations, several Living Blues Awards. It was a glorious return, but it ended suddenly: in July 1997, Allison was diagnosed with inoperable lung cancer. He died a month later (on August 12).

Roy Buchanan never played drums, but the Ozark native, born in 1939, was playing professionally with Dale Hawkins as a teenager and established himself as a guitar legend in Washington, D.C., clubs in the sixties. His first album, the 1972 *Roy Buchanan,* is still a revelation. His 1985 Alligator debut, *When a Guitar Plays the Blues,* won a Grammy nomination, but Buchanan was always a reluctant star (there's a story in print that says he turned down a chance to be a Rolling Stone), and he came to a sad end, hanging himself in a jail cell following a drunk-driving arrest in 1988.

Less successful (so far) but no less interesting is Helena native CeDell Davis, whose unique slide guitar style (he plays the instrument upside down, with his left hand) was developed out of a necessity imposed by a crippling childhood struggle with polio. For ten years in the late 1950s and early 1960s Davis played with Robert Nighthawk, though he's been mostly restricted to a wheelchair since 1957, when he was trampled during a show by patrons of a St. Louis club stampeded by a police raid. Returning to Arkansas, he settled in Pine Bluff, where he played regularly at the Jungle Hut. Though he gained a wider audience in the 1980s with performances as far afield as New York, he didn't record his first album until Fat Possum Records brought out his *Feel Like Doin' Something Wrong* CD (including a Davis interpretation of the old Doc Clayton/Pat Hare outrage, here titled "Murder My Baby") in 1994.

Other Arkansas bluesmen who made careers for themselves in the Chicago blues scene of the 1950s and 1960s include Robert Lowery, from Shuler; "Lazy Bill" Lucas, from Wynne; Emery "Little Junior" Williams, from Haynes; and Robert Woodfork, from Lake Village. Willie Cobbs, a guitar and harmonica player from Monroe, moved to Chicago in 1951 after singing in church choirs and in a spiritual quartet with his brothers in Arkansas. He worked with Little Walter and Muddy Waters and recorded on Memphis labels in the early sixties before resettling in Arkansas around 1970. Brinkley's John Weston never left home, but he's got four albums to his credit—from *So Doggone Blue* in 1992 to *I Tried to Hide from the Blues* in 2001.

Son Seals, CeDell Davis, Luther Allison, the guitarists Lonnie Shields (from West Memphis) and Larry McCray (from Stephens), Michael Burks (born in Milwaukee but with family roots in Camden)—in the hands of such artists as these it would appear that blues music in Arkansas heads into a new century as an old form with a bright future. Broonzy's self-applied title notwithstanding, it would seem that "the last blues singer" is still to be born.

In any consideration of Arkansans in early rock and roll, Henry Glover may be the most important figure of them all. Born in Hot Springs, he started as a trumpet player but left Lucky Millinder's band in the mid-1940s to work as a producer and arranger at King Records, where he handled sessions not only for such blues and R&B artists as John Lee Hooker, Champion Jack Dupree, and James Brown, but also country stars Cowboy Copas and Moon Mullican. Glover produced hits for fellow Arkansans Little Willie John ("Fever") and Wayne Raney ("Why Don't You

Haul Off and Love Me"). In 1956 Glover moved to Roulette, where he worked with Sam and Dave and Joey Dee (he coauthored "Peppermint Twist" in 1961). Best of all, he wrote "Drown in My Own Tears," which found its great performance in Ray Charles's 1956 hit. Levon Helm, writing in 1993, remembered Glover as "a veteran music man" whose encouragement of the young Hawks in 1959 "meant the world to me at the time."[11] Glover died in 1991. Another Arkansan with major credits on the business end of pop music is Little Rock native Al Bell, whose work as vice president at Memphis-based Stax records was crucial to that label's huge success in the 1960s and 1970s.

Things were changing in country music, too. By the 1950s the old radio barn dances were being replaced by television shows with a similar variety format. One of the first and certainly the best known was the *Ozark Jubilee* in Springfield, Missouri, which grew out of various KWTO radio shows, especially the syndicated *Korns-a-Krackin* program that was heard coast to coast on Saturday nights. Down in Little Rock, KLRA's *Barnyard Frolic* show launched the Browns to appearances on both the *Ozark Jubilee* and the *Louisiana Hayride.* A family group from Sparkman, the Browns started as a duo with Jim Ed and older sister Maxine, and later became a trio with the addition of younger sister Bonnie. They started out on KCLA in Pine Bluff before moving to KLRA in 1953. Their 1959 hit, "The Three Bells," took them to national fame, appearances on the *Ed Sullivan Show, American Bandstand,* and additional top-ten hits with "The Old Lamplighter" and "Scarlet Ribbons." In 1963 the Browns joined the cast of the *Grand Ole Opry* where they stayed until their breakup in 1967.[12] Jim Ed went on to a successful solo career, scoring several hit duets with Helen Cornelius between 1976 and 1981.

The Harden Trio, a brother and sister group from the Arkansas England, in Lonoke County, also played the *Barnyard Frolic* before launching a recording career that topped out with "Tippy Toeing," a #3 country hit in 1966. Narvel Felts, a country singer and songwriter from Keiser, won a school talent contest in 1956 with a version of "Blue Suede Shoes" and never looked back. His biggest hit, "Reconsider Me," came in the 1970s, but in the eighties he was still touring, still making country and gospel records. Another big success of the 1970s was Barbara Fairchild, born in

Knobel in 1950—she had a #1 country hit with "Teddy Bear Song" in 1972. Her most recent successes have been in gospel—she released *The Light* in 1991.

A bigger star than any of these was honky-tonk hero Lefty Frizzell, born in Texas but raised in El Dorado. He's best known now for his turbulent career—his given name was William Orville, he earned the "Lefty" with his fists—and his 1959 version of "Long Black Veil," the first hit with that now-perennial weeper (Mick Jagger did it with the Chieftains in 1995). But Frizzell's real high point was the early 1950s, when he had a string of #1 hits beginning with "If You've Got the Money" and "I Love You a Thousand Ways" (written in the Roswell, New Mexico, jail) in 1950.

Frizzell came from a musical family—his younger brother David has also made the charts, first in 1981 with his duet with Shelly West, "You're the Reason God Made Oklahoma" and second with his own barroom classic, "I'm Gonna Hire a Wino to Decorate Our Home" in 1982. Another younger brother who made a successful career in a famous sibling's shadow was Tommy Cash—his top hit was the 1970 tribute number, "Six White Horses." Greenway native "Skeets" McDonald is best remembered now for his 1952 #1 hit, "Don't Let the Stars Get in Your Eyes."

FIGURE 27 The Browns, Bonnie *(top left)*, Jim Ed, Maxine. *Courtesy of Jim Ed Brown*

Little Rock was also home to the first radio station in Arkansas to devote itself to programming aimed at black listeners. KOKY opened in October 1956 and featured R&B and gospel music presented by disc jockeys William "Joy Boy" Jackson and George "TNT" Trueheart. Elvis Presley had played Little Rock eighteen months earlier, appearing at Robinson Auditorium on February 20, 1955, the same year the city acquired a resident rockabilly band in Olen Bingham and the Rhythm Playboys. They played every week at the Hog Drive Inn in North Little Rock, and featured Bingham's mother as the "gal singer," according to piano man Bob Boyd's recollection.[13]

Country music was hit hard by the success of rock and roll in the 1950s, but by the mid-1960s it had made a definite comeback, along with bluegrass, country's old-sounding new cousin. Conway Twitty was hardly alone in finding his way back—Johnny Cash made much the same move, as did Jerry Lee Lewis, the rocker to beat all rockers. (Jerry Lee's rock and roll style is still alive, however, in the frenzied shows of El Dorado's Jason D. Williams.) Ray Charles's 1961 *Modern Sounds in Country and Western Music,* soul versions of classic country songs, was another watershed, as was Bob Dylan's *John Wesley Harding* of 1967. Suddenly, "the country sound was hot, as dozens of noncountry performers . . . trooped south to record ostentatiously country-style music."[14] Patsy Montana had never left, and in 1995 she yodeled and sang about the glories of being a cowgirl's sweetheart in a concert at the Old State House in Little Rock. Charlie Rich and Glen Campbell became big stars; Jimmy Driftwood went from the Snowball school to Nashville; and piano man Floyd Cramer, born in Louisiana but raised in Huttig, had his first big hit in 1958 with "Flip, Flop and Bop." Even T. Texas Tyler was back for a last hit with "Courtin' in the Rain" in 1954 before coming out as a gospel singer and evangelist in 1957. One of the biggest hits of the 1970s, "Mamas, Don't Let Your Sons Grow Up to Be Cowboys," was written by Kaiser native Ed Bruce and his wife, Patsy—Bruce also recorded it first, but the song didn't hit monster status until Waylon and Willie did it in 1978.

Now, as the twenty-first century gets under way, the state has country music stars in figures like Iris DeMent, Ronnie Dunn, Tracy Lawrence, K. T. Oslin, Collin Raye, Lucinda Williams, and newest star Joe Nichols. Dunn, who grew up in El Dorado, is famous as half of Brooks and Dunn,

country's hottest duo act in the early nineties. Raye, born in DeQueen in 1960, also did very well in the 1990s with his *Extremes* CD, which included one cut titled "Little Rock" that actually focused on the Arkansas town (unlike Reba McEntire's song of the same title, which referred to a diamond), while Nichols and Williams were off and running in the new millennium with strong efforts like the 2002 *Man with a Memory* (Nichols) and 2003's *World Without Tears* (Williams). David Lynn Jones, from Bexar, had three albums out by 1992, starting with *Hard Times on Easy Street* in 1987. The 1962 smash hit ballad "Wolverton Mountain" was co-written

FIGURE 28 Jimmy Driftwood *(right)* with his father, Neil Morris. *Courtesy of Special Collections Division, University of Arkansas Libraries, Fayetteville*

and recorded by Louisiana native Claude King, but the mountain was in Van Buren County, where Elijah Wolverton founded a town by opening a post office in his home in 1894, and where the song's star Clifton Clowers, uncle to coauthor Merle Kilgore, did in fact live. In 1981 the state was proud enough of the notoriety to have Governor Frank White declare a "Wolverton Mountain Day." Rogers native Vernon Oxford also had a big hit in 1976 with his "Redneck (The Redneck National Anthem)," and Tracy Lawrence, born in Texas but raised in Foreman and educated at Southern Arkansas University, made a name for himself with *Sticks and Stones* in 1991 and *Alibis* in 1993. Drasco's Melvin Endsley overcame childhood polio to enjoy success in country music, appearing on Searcy's KWCB as a college student and penning hits for Don Gibson ("It Happens Everytime") and Marty Robbins ("Singing the Blues," "Knee Deep in the Blues").

The folk singers, too, continued to prosper. Lee Hays and the Weavers had their biggest successes—in 1950 "Goodnight, Irene," a song they'd learned from Leadbelly, was a big hit, number one on the "Your Hit Parade" show, with the singers each picking up four-figure royalty checks for the first time in their lives. But they also endured bitter defeats—like almost everyone else who ever questioned the achieved perfection of American society at midcentury, Lee Hays and Pete Seeger were hauled before the infamous House Un-American Activities Committee in 1955. Seeger finally quit the group in 1957. He'd been upset for a long time, over everything from wearing tuxedos onstage to performing in posh nightclubs instead of union halls. The last straw seems to have been a cigarette commercial. Erik Darling was brought in to replace him. Hays, who unlike Seeger was broke, had no problem with the commercials; in fact he was soon turning out jingles for Falstaff beer, Betty Crocker pancake mix, and Chock Full o'Nuts doughnuts. Hays died in 1981.

But "Goodnight, Irene" wasn't the only song associated with Leadbelly to make waves after 1950. "The Rock Island Line" was also back in the state in the years after rock and roll. Since 1956, when it was a hit in England for skiffle musician Lonnie Donegan (he got it from Leadbelly, too) the song had become an international hit. The Weavers recorded it for both Decca and Vanguard, though despite Hays's Arkansas ties there is no evidence they associated it with anyone beyond Leadbelly. But Johnny Cash is another story. He recorded "The Rock Island Line" many times, for at least five labels. And then, in 1969, he brought it back where it started. Appearing in concert at Cummins prison, he gave back to the prisoners the song their predecessors had given Lomax and Ledbetter thirty-five years before. A more perfect selection would be hard to imagine. It was a long time coming for such a mighty good road, but the state's most famous train had made it home.

Little Rock native Dan Hicks (born in 1941) started out as a folkie too, before leaping to his future, first in the Charlatans, a pioneering "psychedelic" 1960s San Francisco band, and then, more famously, with the "folk swing" or "folk jazz" inventiveness and wackiness of Dan Hicks and His Hot Licks. Hard to classify but easy to listen to—works like *Where's the Money, Striking It Rich,* and *Last Train to Hicksville* (all from the early seventies) have a secure niche in the Weird Music Hall of Fame.

FIGURE 29 Johnny Cash, 1955. *Reproduced by permission of Getty Images*

Even "The Arkansas Traveler" was back, the oldest song of all—so old that maybe even DeSoto, that conquistador thug, would have garnered a better welcome if he'd known the turn of the tune. But there it was, in 1992, smack on the cover, title of a hot CD by Michelle Shocked, with the star inside backed by Alison Krauss and Union Station, Norman and Nancy Blake, and the Red Clay Ramblers. There was also by this time a new Arkansas song, an unabashed celebration of the state and its people, "Arkansas You Run Deep in Me," written by Little Rock native

Wayland Holyfield for the 150th statehood anniversary celebrations in 1986. Holyfield went from his Mallettown roots to a stellar Nashville songwriting career, penning such hits as George Strait's "Meanwhile" and Don Williams's "You're My Best Friend." Other Arkies making it big in Music City include Little Rock native Steve Dean, who had a hand in Reba McEntire's "Walk On" and Alabama's "Southern Star"; Shawn Camp, from Perryville, who co-wrote "How Long Gone" for Brooks and Dunn and "Two Pina Coladas" for Garth Brooks; and Hampton's Wood Newton, whose "Bobbie Sue" and "Twenty Years Ago" were done by the Oak Ridge Boys and Kenny Rogers.

In the 1950s a very active Arkansas Folklore Society headquartered at the University of Arkansas in Fayetteville hosted annual festivals where singers like Berryville's Fred High and Mary Brisco, Farmington's Doney Hammontree, and Cane Hill's Booth Campbell were featured, and researchers from the university headed by folklore professor Mary Celestia Parler gathered some four thousand songs and instrumental performances between 1949 and 1960. Rackensack Folklore Societies in both Mountain View and Pulaski County sponsored similar festivals from the 1950s into the 1970s, continuing an area tradition going back at least to 1934, when the first of fourteen preliminary regional festivals leading up to the inaugural National Folk Festival in St. Louis was held in Eureka Springs.

Folklorist Bill McNeil, working out of the Ozark Folk Center in Mountain View with Little Rock schoolteacher and musician George West, produced four albums of traditional music between 1981 and 1986, recording Almeda Riddle from Greer's Ferry, Noble Cowden from Cushman, Kenneth Rorie from Batesville, Rance Blankenship from Melbourne, Bob Blair from Mountain View, and the Williams family from Roland. Rodeo rider Glenn Ohrlin, a Minnesota native, had moved to Mountain View in 1954, and was soon both recording and collecting traditional cowboy songs. Ohrlin's *The Hell-Bound Train: A Cowboy Songbook* was published in 1973; a recent album is *The Wild Buckaroo,* a 1983 Rounder release. A 1964 Folkways record, *Music from the Ozarks,* issued recordings made in 1958 by David Mangurian and Donald Hill of Delaney musicians John and Lee Mounce, Calvin Van Brunt, and Danny Patrick. Filmmaker Louis Guida did valuable recording and photodocumentary work with blues and black gospel traditions, publishing a monograph titled *Blues Music in Arkansas* with Lorenzo Thomas and Cheryl Cohen in 1982 and producing the *Keep It to Yourself* album with ten Arkansas blues musicians for the Rooster Blues label in 1983. Jim Borden and Robert Cochran made video documentaries at the University of Arkansas in Fayetteville in 1990 and 1995 starring the Villines Brothers, a gospel group from Newton County, and Fayetteville western swing fiddler Frankie Kelly, and in 1999 Cochran produced *Singing in Zion,* a study of the Zion community tradition centered on the Gilbert family.

Gospel music also continues to flourish in the state. The Brumley festival is probably the state's biggest festival, but gospel quartets and choirs both black and white are active in every county, and Arkansas radio waves carry generous helpings of gospel music (especially in early A.M. and Sunday slots)—in the 1990s, for example, J. C. Love was holding forth on KIPR's *C. and Cee Sunday Morning Gospel* show. Today's biggest names might be Point of Grace (Shelley Breen, Denise Jones, Terry Jones, Heather Payne), who started as students at Ouachita Baptist University and went on to enormous success and fame, producing eight albums and garnering two Grammy nominations and double-figure Dove Awards by 2002. Also at the apex of the gospel firmament these days are the Martins, sisters Joyce and Judy

FIGURE 30 Booth Campbell, Ozark Folk Festival, Eureka Springs, 1952. *Courtesy of Special Collections Division, University of Arkansas Libraries, Fayetteville*

FIGURE 31 Twila Paris.
Courtesy of Old State House Museum Collections, Little Rock

and brother Jonathan, who went from their Hamburg home to a prolific (eight albums as of 2001) and successful career (six Dove Awards and a Grammy nomination). Like Conway Twitty's biographers, Twila Paris's publicity wizards are reluctant to divulge the gospel diva's worldly age, but the Texas-born singer/songwriter worked out of Elm Springs for many years, scoring her first #1 hit in 1984 ("The Warrior Is a Child") and going on to multiple Dove Awards as female vocalist of the year. Russ Taff, who got his start with the Imperials in the 1970s, has also enjoyed considerable success as a solo artist, with at least five Grammys and nine Dove Awards to his credit.

A bit earlier, Gladys McFadden and the Loving Sisters, with ten albums and one Grammy nomination to their credit, enjoyed great success, while Magnolia-born tenor Denver Crumpler starred with the Stamps Melody Boys and the Statesmen until his death in 1957. McFadden got her start doing local radio shows in Lonoke County, and was first recorded on the Houston-based Peacock label in 1962 after members of the Pilgrim Travelers were impressed by what they heard on the radio and helped her make a demo. North Little Rock singer/songwriter Rev. Gerald Thompson scored repeated successes in the 1990s—five albums in a seven-year span, with *Let the Church Say Amen* hitting the #7 spot in 1996.

Other successful groups include the Racy Brothers of Dumas, the Zion Five from Lonoke, and the Gospel Troops from Danville, and Little Rock's Hunter Brothers and the Sensational Revelators of Camden have several CD releases. But the gospel highway is a busy road—the Villines Brothers of Newton County, the Atkins Family of Camden, Pea Ridge's Gospel Carriers, Charles and Pamela Dove of Pine Bluff, the Venable Boys from North Little Rock, Prescott's Frank Rivers, the Merits of Springdale, the Christian Harmonettes of Wynne—a list of the Lord's Arkansas house bands would run to hundreds. Saturday night may be showtime, but Sunday morning takes a backseat to nothing in this state.[15]

It's a long way from fiddlers and ballad singers and church choirs to Elvis in Little Rock, Conway Twitty singing in Russian, Big Bill Broonzy recording in Paris and Copenhagen, and Ronnie Hawkins rocking in Canada. But alongside these spectacular success stories, music in Arkansas carries on today much as it has since territorial times, with local musicians playing for local audiences. Scores of weekly, biweekly, and annual gatherings in community centers, churches, and VFW halls, like the better-known King Biscuit Festival and the Brumley gospel sing continue into the present the spirit of the frontier frolics and hymn singings witnessed by Gerstäcker 150 years ago. In the 1990s, too, there have been annual powwow celebrations that attract dancers and drummers from near and far. The Quapaws and Caddos, five hundred years after DeSoto, are still dancing in Arkansas. The Natural State is now, as it was then, a place with music at its center. In the present as in the past babies fall to sleep on lullabies, and children learn their alphabets in a song that asks approval at its close. Popular hits heard on the radio still aid the courtship dance of tongue-tied adolescents, we graduate and marry to music, and the grief of our funerals is leavened with song.

Consider as a case in point the sad instance of Forester, a small sawmill town in Scott County. It only lasted twenty years—built in 1931, it was closed in 1952—and never had a population much over two thousand. But twenty years is long enough for at least two generations of people to call a place home, and two thousand people in the 1930s and 1940s could sustain a drugstore, an auto dealer, a two-story hotel, and a movie theater that showed mostly cowboy films. There was also, of course, a Forester Band, led by Harry Standerfer, to play for local parties and dances. Housing in the town was rigorously segregated, but both black and white sections had a church shared by Methodist and Baptist congregations. When the black churches hosted singing conventions "visiting choirs converged on Forester, along with hundreds of whites from all over Scott County . . . Groups from the different churches took turns singing, each trying to outdo the others."[16]

Forester has been gone for nearly half a century now, but her former residents and their descendants retain close ties. And in characteristic Arkansas fashion, they have composed their attachments into song. In 1983, at the dedication of a Forester memorial pavilion, "Forester (The Town That Moved Away)" was sung by composer Christine Griffith with the backing of a Waldron band headed by Glen Dale Sparks. In 1987, "Forester, O Forester," described by former resident Jo Parker as "just a little song I wrote one day while missing my childhood," was performed at Billy Roy Wilson Appreciation Day. Billy Roy, by then Judge Wilson, had also lived in Forester.[17]

How, in retrospect, could things have turned out otherwise, could music fail to be at the very center of Arkansas life, even after the days of frontier isolation were a thing of the past? With Memphis and Sam Phillips's Sun recording studio just across the Mississippi to the east, Shreveport's *Louisiana Hayride* right on the southern border, Springfield, Missouri's KWTO programs and the *Ozark Jubilee* to the north, and radio station KVOO and Cain's Academy ballroom, where western swing was always king, to the west in Tulsa, Arkansas was surrounded by a strikingly diverse cross-section of powerful musical influences.

The music showed it too. If Johnny Cash made his name as an early Sun rockabilly artist, his later career made it clear that country and gospel music ran deep in his blood. Charlie Rich would also start with Sun, and later he would be famous as a country singer, but to friends and fellow musicians he would be known first of all for his love of jazz. Stan Kenton would be his particular favorite. Jimmy Driftwood's songs would be huge hits for mainstream country singers, but Driftwood himself would always be devoted to the traditional ballads of the Ozarks. Lucinda Williams and Iris DeMent would make names for themselves as singers and songwriters in Texas, L.A., and Nashville scenes, but Williams's first album would appear on the Folkways label and consist largely of blues covers, while DeMent's songs would work more from country and gospel roots.

Glen Campbell would be everything from a rock guitar ace to a blue-grass picker, and before he was through bluesman Sonny Boy Williamson would make albums with British rockers. Little Junior Parker was an R&B singer, but in 1972 he recorded Willie Nelson's "Funny How Time Slips Away," and "last bluesman" Bill Broonzy covered Tennessee Ernie Ford's "Sixteen Tons" in 1956. Not even Ozark balladeer Ollie Gilbert could escape—in 1965 she mixed a rendition of "Blue Suede Shoes" in

FIGURE 32 Charlie Rich *(right)* with his son Alan, 1975. *Reproduced by permission of Getty Images*

with her old folk songs for California collector D. K. Wilgus. Asked in 1990 where they'd learned their version of "House of the Rising Sun," Mayfield singers Helen Fultz and Phydella Hogan cited the Animals' recording as their favorite.

Long strange trips indeed—but by no means extreme by the standards of the Wonder State, an appropriate present for a past that opened into history with Caddo and Quapaw hosts singing and dancing with French guests. Smackover native Sleepy LaBeef's rockabilly music has taken him from Houston radio shows and cover recordings under various names for Texas border stations to albums for Rounder (based in Massachusetts) and concert performances in England and Spain. In the middle he played a swamp monster in a movie. Ask him about his favorite musicians and he'll tell you about Lefty Frizzell and Rosetta Tharpe and make you listen to tapes of radio preachers.

FIGURE 33 Sleepy La Beef. *Courtesy of Webb Chappell, Rounder Records*

In 1982 LaBeef attempted to demonstrate beyond doubt the reality of demonic possession to skeptical university types in Fayetteville by playing a cassette from the vast collection he carried with him in his Cobra motor home. In went the tape, and out came static-filled rant, the last days harangue of a holiness preacher. It was heavy stuff, and we were impressed. But finally, we thought, we'd heard it before, too many times, a mix of apocalypse, paranoia, bitterness, the old peckerwood resentment recognized long ago by Mencken as driven by the overriding fear that somebody somewhere was having a good time. It was, Sleepy then told us, clinching his point, the voice of Jim Jones, already on the down-bound train headed for Cyanide Station, and the Devil himself was the engineer. Sleepy LaBeef—rockabilly baritone, Rosetta Tharpe and Lefty Frizzell fan, theologian of last days, Arkansas music man. We who listened were both entertained and instructed.

Something of the old ballad impulse is still alive, too, the same that produced songs about Jesse James and the Battles of Pea Ridge and Prairie Grove more than a century ago. Now they deal with contemporary events, and most of them are ephemeral creations, soon forgotten. But what's not ephemeral and has not changed is the impulse to preserve important events by casting them into the memorable form of song. When a Missouri farmer was briefly notorious in 1981 for breaking into the elevators of a bankrupt company to get his own soybeans back, he inspired a pair of Jonesboro musicians to compose and record "The Ballad of Wayne Cryts." "Resurrection Sunday," in 1978, was another 45 rpm issue that immortalized the case of Gladys Rogers of Harrison, who after her death at eighty was packed in dry ice by her son. He planned to bring her back by prayer, and he evidently kept at it for six weeks, even transporting Mom to a mortuary in Missouri to escape Arkansas authorities. The opening stanza gets right down to business: "In a little town way down in the Ozarks / Came a man to raise his mother from the dead / She was setting all alone in a deep freeze / Just waiting for the Lord to raise the lid."[18] Even more recent is the 1995 "Oh White River," written and recorded by Durham resident Tommy Hansen as part of a campaign against a proposed landfill on nearby Hobbs Mountain. The country and its creatures are beautiful, Hansen sings, but "to keep them in this natural state / the landfill's got to go."[19]

In 1972 Almeda Riddle, living in Cleburne County, recorded *Ballads and Hymns from the Ozarks* for Rounder while Black Oak Arkansas, working out of their "heaven in the Ozarks" commune eighty miles away in Marion County, was producing *Raunch 'n' Roll/Live*. Meanwhile, Huntsville's own Ronnie Hawkins—back flipping, camel walking—was performing for Queen Elizabeth up in Canada.

It all seems mightily bizarre, a rich mixture strange beyond imagining, unless you come from Arkansas. Here, amid such fertile combining, is a picture to end with, to call at least a coda to send us back again to the music. It's a huge family portrait poised in the mind, the music makers gathered against the green background of their land. Arkansas itself fills the frame, the whole green state in all its variety, Ozark highlands along the Buffalo River to the lush flatlands of the Grand Prairie, piney woods of the Gulf Plain to the rich bottomlands of the Mississippi Delta. Time is compressed in this mind's-eye tableau—against this varied landscape's background Emma Dusenbury stands next to Peetie Wheatstraw, the great folk singer in her poor woman's flour-sack dress and the High Sheriff of Hell resplendent in his spiffy suit. Jim Dandy, shirtless in outrageous Spandex, poses by a guitar-wielding Rosetta Tharpe, while buckskin-clad

FIGURE 34 Ronnie Hawkins *(at right)* with Carl Perkins *(center)* and Ray Davies. *Reproduced by permission of Getty Images*

Friedrich Gerstäcker enjoys the yodeling of cowgirl Patsy Montana. Everyone is here, old and young, famous and obscure. Not one is missing, though no list can name them all.

JoJo Thompson, Bing Cunningham, Josh Altheimer—fine piano men. Buddy Hayes, Ronnie Hawkins's mentor. Bookmiller Shannon and Clarke Buehling, banjo pickers, and a horde of famous fiddlers—Cotton Combs, Polk County's Ruel Bain, Tommy Henderson, Willie Morrison, the flamboyant Violet Hensley. Bluesmen Little Willie Anderson, Sammy Lawhorn, Buster Benton, Calvin Leavy. Brenda Patterson, a gritty singer identified as Arkansan on an old LP cover, and "Sarge" West, singing fine country music in Springdale. Reola Jackson and Mack White, Parker Mountain Bluegrass, and Stuttgart's John Dillon with the Ozark Mountain Daredevils. All the gospel groups, black and white, the old shape note and Sacred Harp singers and the bright new groups with their electric guitars and keyboards—the Ward Boys, Joe Jones and the Supreme Angels, the Home State Quartet and the Melody Boys, Jessie Mae Blair and Nesbit Souter, the Word Singers and the Gospel Harmonettes, Jimmy McKissic, Denise Lemons, the Austin Franks Quartet, and the Atkins Family.

On and on they come, a vast assembly. Folkies cheek by jowl with bar bands and bluegrass outfits—Crow Johnson, Jed Clampitt, Lark In the Morning, Still On the Hill and Richard Johnson with Zorro and the Blue Footballs, Sugarhill, Greasy Greens, and Paper Hearts. The new music types, the punks, Goths, and bizarrely named grunge bands, yesterday's heroes and tomorrow's stars jumbled together—Be, B-Side, Charred Barbies, Delta Angels, Dreamfast, Gunbunnies, Haphazard, Ho Hum, Kicks, Malls, Mulehead, Pokerface, Silence the Epilogue, Smiley Died, Starkz, Techno-Squid Eats Parliament, Trusty. The whole crowd busy keeping the blues alive—Lucious Spiller, Blind Boy White, Gone For Good Morgan, Oreo Blue. From oldest to newest— Essie Whitman and Ollie Gilbert to Jason Morphew and Evanescence (Amy Lee and Joe Nichols may be the state's most successful stars in 2004).

FIGURE 35 Joe Nichols. *Courtesy of Joe Nichols*

Everybody from the endless list, the Quapaw with his rattle to the latest green-hair wildman got fifteen rings and pins stuck through his skin. You call your sound a song, you're welcome here.

So: end with homecoming, reunion, dinner on the grounds. Everybody back home in Arkansas—all the gifted people in this lovely place, every song that delights and consoles us, each tune that solaces our defeats, shreds our pretensions, assaults our shortcomings, or simply makes us dance. They're basic as breeze and birdsong, heart's steady pulse or breath's sibilant whisper. In between, poised between weather and physiology, touching on both, created by people reaching out to other people—that's music, these sweet sounds that cadence our lives.

FIGURE 36 Ronnie Hawkins and the Hawks—*from left,* Jerry Penfound, Ronnie Hawkins, Levon Helm, Rick Danko, Robbie Robertson. *Courtesy of Ronnie Hawkins and Ronnie Hawkins Promotions*

Black Oak Arkansas

Made up of five young men from the delta counties of northeast Arkansas, Black Oak Arkansas enjoyed great popularity in the 1970s as particularly uncompromising exponents of the "redneck rock" made popular by groups like Lynyrd Skynyrd, ZZ Top, and the Charlie Daniels Band. Band leader Jim Mangrum was in fact from Black Oak, while sidemen Rick Reynolds, Pat Daugherty, Stanley Knight, and Harvey Jett came from Manila, Jonesboro, Bono, and Marion.

They'd been playing together since 1964, but when Stax issued their first album in 1969 they were calling themselves the Knowbody Else. After moving to L.A. and signing with Atlantic they toured relentlessly in support of *Black Oak Arkansas* in 1970, *Keep the Faith* and *If an Angel Came to See You* in 1972, and *Raunch 'n' Roll Live* in 1973. The payoff came in 1974, when *High on the Hog* became their first gold album and they toured England opening for Black Sabbath.

Through it all they gained a loyal following centered on blue-collar southern white males while offending liberals with their Confederate flags and guns, conservatives with their long hair, dope, and communal living, and authorities everywhere by the violence that seemed to accompany far too many of their shows. So virulent was the opposition that the band sued Harrison preacher J. D. Tedder in 1976 after he called them a "mongrel group of satanic origins promoting drugs, sex, revolution." Black Oak won the suit, but was awarded only one dollar in damages.

Elton Britt

James Elton Baker was born in Zack in 1913 to Irish and Cherokee parents. After his discovery by scouts for the *Beverly Hillbillies* show as a singer, guitar player, and "boy yodeler" in 1930, he moved to California to launch a career in music and films. Over his long career he recorded nearly seven hundred singles and fifty-six albums for RCA Victor (he also

FIGURE 37 Black Oak
Arkansas. *Courtesy of
Butch Stone*

recorded for several other labels), wrote songs, appeared in several movies, starred on the *Grand Ole Opry* and the *WVVA Jamboree,* and hosted *The Elton Britt Show* on ABC television. Like his fellow Arkansan Patsy Montana, Britt was one of country music's finest yodelers—he sometimes billed himself as the "highest yodeler in the world." "Chime Bells," one of his own compositions, is a determined attempt to make good on such a claim.

Britt's greatest hit was the 1942 patriotic smash, "There's a Star-Spangled Banner Waving Somewhere," which tells the pathetic story of a would-be soldier prevented by a "crippled leg" from realizing his dream of becoming one of "Uncle Sam's great heroes" and helping "take the Axis down a peg." The song sold a million and a half copies in its first year; by 1960 it was up to four million. Britt's combination of patriotism and commercial savvy was still going strong during the Korean conflict, when he weighed in with "The Red That We Want Is the Red We've Got (In the Old Red, White, and Blue)." Britt died in 1972.

William "Big Bill" Broonzy

Born in Scott, Mississippi, in 1893, William Lee Conley Broonzy grew up on a farm near Pine Bluff, where a maternal uncle, Jerry Belcher, taught him to play violin on a homemade instrument. He played as a boy and young man for area churches and picnics before serving in the U.S. Army in World War I. After a brief career in Little Rock clubs in 1919–1920, Broonzy moved to Chicago, where his 1928 hit, "Big Bill's Blues," launched a career as a vocalist and more especially as an innovative guitarist that soon made him one of that city's best-known musicians.

On December 23, 1938, he appeared in John Hammond's famous "Spirituals to Swing" concerts at New York's Carnegie Hall as a last-minute substitute when Robert Johnson couldn't be located. (As it turned out Johnson had been dead since August, poisoned by a jealous husband at a house party near Greenwood, Mississippi.) In the years before the Second World War Broonzy became a regular on the New York "folk"

FIGURE 38 Elton Britt.
Courtesy of Old State House Museum Collections, Little Rock

FIGURE 39 Bill Broonzy, circa 1935. *Reproduced by permission of Getty Images*

circuit where his acoustic performances of gospel and folk songs mixed in with blues made him popular with new, mostly white audiences.

The same show proved equally successful in England, Europe, Africa, South America, and Australia, where from 1951 to 1957 Broonzy toured regularly, billing himself as "the last blues singer alive" even as a vibrant postwar blues scene was developing back in Chicago. Broonzy died of cancer in 1958, leaving more than three hundred recordings as a featured artist and many more as a guitar accompanist for Washboard Sam (his half-brother), John Lee Williamson, and others. Many of his later recordings were made in Europe—in Milan, Copenhagen (where in 1956 he recorded "Sixteen Tons," the Merle Travis coal-mining ballad that had been a number-one hit for Tennessee Ernie Ford at the end of 1955), Paris, and London, among other cities. When Broonzy did return to Chicago in the 1950s, he came not as a bluesman to the old clubs, but as a "folk singer" appearing in concert with Pete Seeger. Among the many titles recorded over this long period is at least one—"Back to Arkansas"—that ties him to his old home state.

Albert E. Brumley

Albert Brumley was born near Spiro, Oklahoma, on October 29, 1905. In 1922 his chance attendance at a rural singing school gave him his life's vocation. When the teacher wrote a scale on the chalkboard and explained that all songs ever written were contained within it, the boy was thrilled and galvanized. "That set me afire," he said.

MELODY FOUR
HARRISON, ARK.

ALBERT E. BRUMLEY	HUGH TAYLOR	CLAY RICHESIN	EVERETT CONE	TILDON DART
PIANIST	1ST TENOR	2ND TENOR	BARITONE	BASS

In 1926 Brumley took a bus to Hartford, Arkansas, and enrolled at Eugene M. Bartlett's Hartford Musical Institute, a branch of Bartlett's gospel music songbook publishing company. By 1929 he was touring as a bass singer and piano player with the Hartford Quartet and leading his own singing schools using Hartford songbooks. In Powell, Missouri, at one of these schools, he found a wife—Goldie Edith Schell later claimed that she knew at once that "he would be a great songwriter and I just wanted to help him." The couple married in 1931, settled in Powell, and eventually raised six children.

Brumley's most famous song, "I'll Fly Away," was first published in Bartlett's 1932 collection, *The Wonderful Message.* He eventually wrote

FIGURE 40 Melody Four.
Courtesy of Albert E. Brumley and Sons

more than eight hundred songs, an impressive total even in a field known for prolific composers. No other title achieved the renown of "I'll Fly Away," but many Brumley numbers, including "I Will Meet You in the Morning," "Rank Strangers to Me," and "Turn Your Radio On," remain popular with gospel singers and audiences. Another Brumley composition, "Nobody Answered Me," was sung so often by *Grand Ole Opry* star Roy Acuff that many assumed he'd written it. Brumley's songs have been recorded by scores of artists, ranging from Elvis Presley to Aretha Franklin, Ray Charles to Loretta Lynn. Brumley's stature in the gospel music field is comparable to that of the great African American composer and promoter Thomas A. Dorsey. Brumley died in 1977.

Sonny Burgess

Sonny Burgess was born May 28, 1931, in Newport. He grew up with country music—his first guitar was a mail-order Gene Autry model from Sears & Roebuck—but turned to blues and R&B as a teenager. His first professional appearances exhibit this variety—one was a Hadacol Medicine Show headlined by harmonica stars Wayne Raney and Lonnie Glosson, another was a stint as lead guitarist for country act Freddie Hart, a third was as the opening act for a 1955 Elvis Presley show in Newport when Burgess was fronting a band called the Moonlighters.

His defining moment came in 1956 when Sam Phillips released "Red Headed Woman" on his soon-to-be-famous Sun label. Burgess and his band, the Pacers, astounded early rockabilly concert crowds with their frenzied shows—Burgess himself was a lurid flame, decked from head to toe in demonic red, including shoes and socks, dyed hair, and red guitar.

Burgess never had a national hit, and between 1968 and 1984 he played and recorded only rarely, but the pioneering rockabilly sides still held their appeal, appearing on several anthologies and box sets, including *We Wanna Boogie* (1990) and *Sonny Burgess* (1996) on the Rounder label. In 1984 and 1985 Burgess played festivals in England and joined the Sun Rhythm Section in the late 1980s, playing regularly through the mid-1990s. In 1991 the Bear Family label issued a two-CD set of his complete Sun sides, and in 1992 he issued an album of new material, *Tennessee Border*. Burgess continues to perform regularly.

FIGURE 41 Sonny Burgess.
Courtesy of Bobby Crawford

Glen Campbell

Born in 1938 in Delight, Glen Campbell got his start in music at four when his father paid five dollars for a Sears & Roebuck guitar. By the age of fourteen he'd learned banjo and mandolin too, and had dropped out of school to play professionally in his uncle Dick Bills's band in New Mexico.

Campbell's first record was a modest hit in 1961, "Turn Around, Look at Me," which earned him a contract with Capitol Records. At first he was featured as an instrumentalist, with albums titled *Big Bluegrass Special* (1962), *The Astounding 12-String Guitar of Glen Campbell* (1964), and *Big Bad Rock Guitar of Glen Campbell* (1965). All this changed with the first blockbuster vocal hits in 1967, when both "Gentle on My Mind" and "By the Time I Get to Phoenix" went to the top of the charts and earned

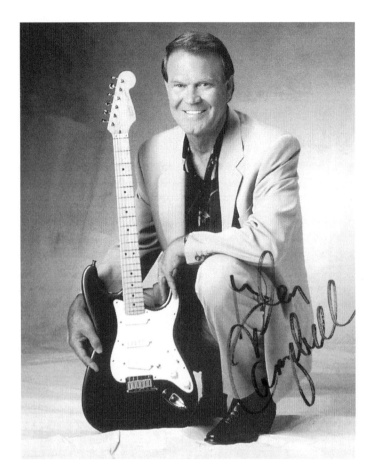

Campbell four Grammy Awards. Television and movies came next—in 1969 he appeared with John Wayne in *True Grit,* and *The Glen Campbell Goodtime Hour* began a four-year run on CBS.

Meanwhile, the hits kept coming: "Galveston," "Dreams of an Everyday Housewife," "Wichita Lineman," "Rhinestone Cowboy." The albums did equally well—by 1978 twelve albums had made gold, five had gone platinum, and one was double platinum. The man from Delight had done it all—played for the Queen of England in 1972 and set up his own golf tournament, the Glen Campbell Los Angeles Open, on the PGA tour. Among the thirty-seven albums issued by Capitol is one from 1973 entitled *Arkansas.*

FIGURE 42 Glen Campbell. *Courtesy of Glen Campbell*

Johnny Cash

John R. Cash was born in Kingsland in 1932, the fourth child and third son of Ray and Carrie Rivers Cash. In 1935 the family moved to Dyess, a federal resettlement project located on sixteen thousand acres of swampland in Mississippi County. "I grew up under socialism," Cash quipped later. Both sides of the family were devoted to music—Mrs. Cash's father taught a singing school, and one of the first "luxuries" she purchased for their new home was a battery-powered radio, acquired in 1936, which allowed the family to listen to the *Grand Ole Opry* and to their favorite Carter Family hymns broadcast over the powerful stations on the Mexican border.

Johnny Cash graduated from the Dyess High School in 1950, and worked briefly in Detroit before enlisting in the U.S. Air Force, where he served in Germany until 1954. His older brother Roy had formed a band, the Delta Rhythm Ramblers, in the late 1930s, but Johnny Cash got his first break when Sam Phillips's Sun label issued "Hey Porter" and "Cry, Cry, Cry" in June 1955. In 1956 "I Walk the Line," still Cash's best-known song, was released, he became a regular member of the *Opry* in the same year, and soon went on, like other early Sun artists Elvis Presley, Carl Perkins, Jerry Lee Lewis, and Roy Orbison, to a fame that went far beyond these regional beginnings.

In December 1957, for example, the release of "Ballad of a Teenage

FIGURE 43 Johnny Cash. *Reproduced by permission of Getty Images*

Queen" was backed by a whirlwind fifteen-day Canadian tour featuring a Teenage Queen contest in each city. (A young Joni Mitchell, already writing songs of her own, was crowned in Saskatoon.) In 1958 Cash signed with Columbia; in 1968 his *Johnny Cash at Folsom Prison* was one of the first successful live-performance albums, and as late as 2002 Johnny Cash was still making the charts and garnering rave reviews with *American Recordings* (1994). Cash died in 2003.

The Cate Brothers Band

When Earl and Ernie Cate formed their first band in Springdale in the early 1960s, they called themselves the Del Rays. By 1970 they were the Cates Gang, regulars on the Dickson Street and frat party circuit in Fayetteville, and the MetroMedia label had issued their first album, *Wanted.* After a second MetroMedia release, *Come Back Home,* the group was signed by Elektra-Asylum for three mid-1970s albums—*The Cate Bros.* in 1975, *The Cate Bros. Band* in 1977, and *In One Eye and Out the Other* in 1978. They also did one album for Atlantic, *Fire on the Tracks,* in 1979. The band in this period consisted of Earl and Ernie on guitar and keyboards, Terry Cagle on drums, and Ron Eoff on bass.

By the 1990s the Cates had twenty-five years of playing and recording under their belts, including sessions with everybody from Bob Dylan and the Grateful Dead to KoKo Taylor and the Beach Boys. When fellow Arkansan William Jefferson Clinton ascended to the White House in 1992, the Cates were on hand to help him boogie the inaugural night away. Only Earl and Ernie remained from the

1970s band, but a new lineup had been together five years when they released *Radioland* in 1995, and included Porky Hill on drums, John Davies on bass, and David Renko on saxophone. *Struck a Vein* was released in 1997, followed by *The Cate Brothers Band Live* in 1999. The Cate Brothers Band continues to perform regularly in their home territory; the latest lineup includes Ron Eoff on bass and drummer Mickey Eoff, who came on board following the death of Porky Hill in 2000.

Iris DeMent

Iris DeMent was born in 1961 in Paragould, the youngest of fourteen children. The family was musical—her mother "let me turn the records up real loud, and she'd sing with me on the records," and her father was a fiddler who played for neighborhood dances until he got saved and felt obliged to put his fiddle aside. Her older sisters had a group, the DeMent Sisters, who once sang backup on a gospel record. "My parents stuck to gospel music," DeMent wrote. "The first record I remember is a Loretta Lynn record of gospel songs my mother used to play."

FIGURE 45 Iris DeMent. *Reproduced by permission from Mark Tucker, Warner Bros. Records, Inc.*

In 1964 the family moved to California, where DeMent lived until she was seventeen. While living in Topeka, Kansas, she wrote her first song at twenty-five, and soon after moved to Kansas City, where she began singing at "open mike" nights in local clubs. Another move took her to Nashville, but by 1991 she was back in Kansas City, where she now lives.

Infamous Angel came out on the Rounder label in 1992, backed by words of praise from John Prine and supporting vocals by Emmylou Harris, Hal Ketchum, and Flora Mae DeMent, Iris's mother. Nine of the eleven cuts were written by

DeMent, but the album closed with the traditional gospel favorite "Higher Ground." *My Life,* issued by Warner Brothers in 1994, is dedicated to her father, who died in 1992, and offers more of the same. The sound is country gospel, and eight of the ten songs are DeMent originals.

Jimmy Driftwood

James Corbett Morris was born in 1907 near Mountain View. After graduating from Marshall High School and Arkansas State Teacher's College in Conway, he taught in Arkansas and Louisiana schools. His most famous song, "The Battle of New Orleans," written as a teaching aid for history classes, became a #1 hit for country singer Johnny Horton in 1959, though in 1958 Driftwood had recorded his own much longer version on his first album. The Horton version sold over five million copies and was voted best song of the year. Another Driftwood composition, "The Tennessee Stud," was a hit for Eddy Arnold in 1959, and Driftwood himself was soon appearing regularly on the *Grand Ole Opry.*

In 1962, back home in Arkansas, he founded the Rackensack Folklore Society to encourage the musical traditions of the Ozarks, and soon thereafter devoted himself to the establishment of the Ozark Folk Center in Mountain View, serving for a time as music coordinator after the facility opened in 1973. Driftwood also made several international tours for the U.S. Department of State, and served on the Arkansas State Parks Commission. He produced an album of Ozark folk music for the National Geographic Society in 1972, and was also active in the campaign to establish a national park along the Buffalo River. Driftwood died in 1998.

FIGURE 46 Jimmy Driftwood. *Courtesy of Arkansas History Commission, Little Rock*

Emma Dusenbury

Born in the north Georgia hill country in 1862, Emma Hays came to Arkansas in 1872, staying first in Crittenden County before traveling to Batesville by steamboat in February 1873, where the family was taken by ox wagon to settle near Gassville in Baxter County.

Sometime after 1880 she moved to Marion County, near Yellville, where she married Ernest (or Earnest) Dusenbury. Two years later the couple had their only child, a daughter they named Ora. Soon after this, when Ora was two years old, Dusenbury went blind. After living a wandering life for approximately fifteen years, supporting themselves by picking cotton and by Mr. Dusenbury's work on railroads, in packing houses, and various other jobs, the family settled on a small farm near Mena. It was there, in about 1928, that her vast knowledge of traditional song was first appreciated, initially by F. M. Goodhue, a teacher at nearby Commonwealth College, and soon afterward by Vance Randolph, John

FIGURE 47 Emma Dusenbury. *Courtesy of Special Collections Division, University of Arkansas Libraries, Fayetteville*

Gould Fletcher, Laurence Powell, Sidney Robertson, and other collectors. Eventually, in 1936, Dusenbury recorded more than one hundred songs for the Archive of American Folk Song in the Library of Congress. John A. Lomax, the best known of the collectors, remembered in his autobiography that she sang "almost continuously" for two days, and contributed the greatest number of traditional ballads "ever recorded from one person, so far as I know." In the same year, in her only brush with fame, she sang in Little Rock as a part of the celebration of the one hundredth anniversary of Arkansas statehood. In what must rank as the state's most spectacular instance of high-culture/low-culture exchange, five of

Dusenbury's tunes were used by composer Laurence Powell, organizer of the Little Rock symphony orchestra, for "An Arkansas Rondo." Dusenbury died in 1941.

Lefty Frizzell

William Orville Frizzell was born March 31, 1928, in Corsicana, Texas. He grew up in various Arkansas, east Texas, and Louisiana oil towns, and got his nickname in a schoolboy fight. He fell in love with Jimmie Rodgers records early on, and was barely into his teens when he started performing regularly on local radio shows and talent contests. In 1945 he married Alice Harper and settled in Roswell, New Mexico, where he found regular work at radio station KGFL and a club called the Cactus Garden.

FIGURE 48 Lefty Frizzell. *Courtesy of Country Music Hall of Fame® and Museum, Walden Fabry Collection*

After serving a six-month term for statutory rape in 1947–1948, Frizzell gave up on music for a while (though he continued to write songs, and auditioned without success with the *Louisiana Hayride*). He lived for a time in El Dorado, worked in the Texas oil fields, and settled again in Big Spring, Texas, singing at the Ace of Clubs. His big break came in 1950, when his first recording for Columbia ("If You've Got the Money I've Got the Time" and "I Love You a Thousand Ways") was a two-sided #1 hit.

After that he was a star, though he continued to be troubled by heavy drinking and young women (he was arrested backstage at the *Grand Ole Opry* in 1951 on a charge of contributing to delinquency). The hits continued into the late 1950s and 1960s: "Long Black Veil" was a smash in 1959 and remains popular; "Saginaw, Michigan" was his last #1 hit in 1964. Merle Haggard, George Jones, Randy Travis, and George Strait, among others, have credited his influence. Frizzell died in 1975, and was elected to the Country Music Hall of Fame in 1982.

Al Green

Born in 1946 in Forrest City, Al Green began singing in a gospel group with his older brothers before he was twelve. His style was much influenced by Sam Cooke, and he had a modest hit in 1967 with "Back Up Train." But it wasn't until 1970, when he teamed with producer Willie Mitchell at Hi Records in Memphis, that he enjoyed sustained success—"I Can't Get Next to You" in late 1970 was a hit, while "Tired of Being Alone" (at #11 on the pop list) and "Let's Stay Together" (at #1 on both pop and R&B) in 1971 were bigger still. The big 1972 hit, "I'm Still in Love with You," earned Green Best R&B Vocalist Awards from *Billboard* and *Cash Box*.

In 1974, ten years after his idol Cooke had been murdered in not dissimilar circumstances, Green was seriously injured when an unhappy girl-

FIGURE 49 Al Green. *Reproduced by permission of Getty Images*

friend showered him with boiling grits before doing an even better job on herself with a gun. Recovered from his burns, Green turned increasingly to gospel music. In 1976 he was ordained as a minister, and for the last fifteen years has pastored his own Full Gospel Tabernacle in Memphis. "Just go to Hale and turn left," he tells callers who would visit. By 1980 he had turned away from soul music to record several top-selling gospel albums, though he still took time out from ministerial duties to tour in this country and abroad, and in the 1990s he continued to work the edges of the pop/gospel boundary.

Reverend Green was voted into the Rock and Roll Hall of Fame in 1995.

Ronnie Hawkins

FIGURE 50 Ronnie Hawkins. *Courtesy of Ronnie Hawkins and Ronnie Hawkins Promotions*

Ronnie Hawkins was born in Huntsville in 1935. His mother was a schoolteacher and his father was a barber. He learned gospel music and ballads from his grandmother and country tunes from his paternal uncle Delmer, who played on the *Louisiana Hayride* in Shreveport. In 1945 the family moved to Fayetteville, where Hawkins was introduced to blues by Buddy Hayes, a jazz trumpet player who shined shoes in the shop where his father worked.

After brief stints as a student at the University of Arkansas and a soldier in the U.S. Army, Hawkins moved to Helena in 1957 to assemble a band. Within the year they were in Canada, where Hawkins would hold forth for years as Ronnie Hawkins and the Hawks from Le Coq D'Or in Toronto, introducing audiences to high-octane rock 'n' roll (his act in those years included onstage backflips and a "camel walk" by the lead singer), encouraging Canadian musicians, and throwing infamous afterhours parties that, in Hawkins's own phrasing, "Nero would be ashamed to attend."

The big flirtation with fame came in 1959, when Roulette put out two singles that made the charts—"Forty Days" climbed to #45, and "Mary Lou" did better, reaching #26. Albums followed—*Ronnie Hawkins* in 1959, *Mr. Dynamo, Folk Ballads of Ronnie Hawkins,* and *Ronnie Hawkins Sings the Songs of Hank*

Williams in 1960—but stardom proved elusive. By late 1963, when one set of Hawks went out on their own and became the Band, Hawkins simply put together a new group and kept on rocking. He's almost seventy now, been in the movies, been to the White House, still rocking.

Levon Helm

Mark Lavon Helm was born in 1940 in Elaine. His mother sang at home and his father played guitar in a local house party band, but it was a live show by Bill Monroe and His Blue Grass Boys (then featuring Lester Flatt and Earl Scruggs) in Marvell in 1946 that marked "the end of cowboys and Indians" for the six-year-old in the audience. "I was hooked," he said. Later appearances by the F. S. Walcott Rabbit Foot Minstrels and "our local musical hero" Sonny Boy Williamson only intensified the commitment. By the early 1950s he was appearing regularly in school and county fair talent contests with his sister, and catching the just-emerging Elvis Presley at club and high school dates in Helena and Marianna. When Ronnie Hawkins arrived in 1957, impressive in a duck-tail haircut and looking for a drummer, Helm was ready.

The rest is music history—six years working with Hawkins, going out with the other Hawks in 1963 to form the Band, the work with Bob Dylan and the move to Woodstock leading to the breakthrough *Music from Big Pink* album in 1968, followed by *The Band* in 1969 and five additional albums. In 1976, the Band broke up after a final concert chronicled on film in *The Last Waltz* (1978). For Helm there was another band—the RCO All-Stars—more albums, a tour of Japan, and a new career as a film and television actor with roles in *Coal Miner's Daughter* and *The Dollmaker*. In 1983 the Band reformed and ten years later, surviving even the suicide of Richard Manuel, produced *Jericho* (1993), with a title cut every bit as commanding, if not as famous, as "The Night They Drove Old Dixie Down."

Howlin' Wolf

Chester Arthur Burnett was born June 10, 1910, near West Point, Mississippi. His parents were farmers. In 1923 the family moved to the Ruleville area, near the Dockery plantation, where Burnett was inspired by the music of Charlie Patton. He started playing professionally around 1930, already billing himself as Howlin' Wolf. (Stories vary as to the name's origin—he got it from a bluesman named J. T. Smith, who recorded a song titled "Howlin' Wolf" in the 1930s; he got it for his combination of huge frame and shouting style.)

Except for a four-year stint in the army from 1941 to 1945 (he never went overseas), Wolf spent the 1930s and 1940s farming in Mississippi and Arkansas. In 1948, living in West Memphis with his second wife (his first wife, a sister of blues singer Willie Brown, died soon after their marriage), he began appearing regularly on KWEM. In 1951 he was recorded by Sam Phillips at the Memphis Recording Service (soon to become Sun Records) and by Ike Turner. Records were issued on Chicago's Chess label (the Phillips recordings) and on Los Angeles's Modern (the Turner recordings); contractual disputes followed, with Wolf eventually remaining with Chess.

FIGURE 52 Howlin' Wolf *(at left)*, Chicago, circa 1955. *Reproduced by permission of Getty Images*

Wolf also had a regular radio show on Forrest City's station KXJK in 1952, but soon moved to Chicago, where he continued to record regularly at Chess into the 1970s, eventually cutting over one hundred songs. Many of his songs have become blues and R&B standards—"How Many More Years," "Smokestack Lightnin'," "Moanin' at Midnight," among others. Wolf was a uniquely powerful vocalist and an enormously influential figure in the development of an urban R&B music rooted in rural blues. Wolf died in 1976.

Scott Joplin

Scott Joplin's birth date is uncertain. He was born near Marshall, Texas, in 1867 or 1868, and grew up in Texarkana on both sides of the

FIGURE 53 Scott Joplin. *Courtesy of the Butler Center for Arkansas Studies, Central Arkansas Library System*

Arkansas/Texas border. Julius Weiss, a local music teacher, noticed his precocious talent (he first played piano at seven, in the home of a family where his mother worked) and introduced him to classical music and opera.

Joplin moved to Sedalia, Missouri, in the 1880s, and made it his primary home until 1901, despite frequent travels, playing with the Queen City Cornet Band and studying music at George R. Smith College. He also performed regularly at the Maple Leaf Club and the Black 400 Club. In 1899 his "Maple Leaf Rag" became the most successful piano rag of the era.

In 1901 Joplin moved to St. Louis, where by 1903 he had completed his first ragtime opera, *A Guest of Honor* (now lost). In 1904 he married a nineteen-year-old Freddie Alexander in Little Rock only to lose her to pneumonia just months later. In 1911, after moving to New York, Joplin published his second opera, the now-celebrated *Treemonisha* (though he never saw it performed). Joplin's final years were difficult—he died in 1917 in a mental hospital in New York City—but his posthumous fame has been enormous; *Treemonisha* was given its first full performance in 1972, and the use of his music in the 1974 hit movie *The Sting* made him more famous with the general public (especially for "The Entertainer," a rag first published in 1902) than he'd ever been in his lifetime. By 1983 he was on a U.S. postage stamp.

Louis Jordan

Louis Jordan was born July 8, 1908, in Brinkley. He studied clarinet and saxophone with his father, music teacher and bandleader Jimmy Jordan. He was playing in Dad's band, the Rabbit Foot Minstrels, while he was still in high school. By 1929 he was on the road as a professional musician, playing alto and soprano saxophone (and occasionally singing) for Jimmy Pryor's Imperial Serenaders, Chick Webb, Fats Waller, Jim Winters, and other bands.

In 1938 he put together his own band, the soon-to-be-famous Tympany Five. By 1939 he was embarked on a fifteen-year recording career with Decca, producing an impressive array of hits during the war years—many of them still well known ("Caldonia," "Five Guys Named Moe," "Is You Is or Is You Ain't My Baby," and "Choo, Choo, Ch'Boogie," among others). The Tympany Five also appeared in several Hollywood films between 1944 and 1948.

In the immediate postwar years, Jordan and the Tympany Five were as popular as any band in the country, racking up fifty-five top-ten R&B singles between 1942 and 1951. He was a great

FIGURE 54 Louis Jordan, circa 1950. *Reproduced by permission of Getty Images*

showman and an enormously versatile musician, rooted in blues and jazz but also extremely successful as a crooner, a scat singer, a balladeer, and a comedian. He later recorded with Ella Fitzgerald, Bing Crosby, and Louis Armstrong—the collaboration of Jordan and Armstrong on "You Rascal You" is a great moment in musical goofing. Jordan's showmanship also inspired early rock and rollers like Little Richard, Fats Domino, and Chuck Berry. Jordan died in 1975.

Albert King

Albert King was born Albert Nelson on April 25, 1923, in Indianola, Mississippi. His father was a preacher, his mother sang church music, and the son did his first singing in Mississippi churches. Moving with

FIGURE 55 Albert King.
Courtesy of Old State House Museum Collections, Little Rock

his family to Arkansas in the early 1930s, King learned to play guitar and by 1940 was playing roadhouses in the Osceola area. In the late 1940s and early 1950s he was still active as a gospel singer, traveling as far afield as South Bend, Indiana, with a gospel group called the Harmony Kings Gospel Quartet.

King made his first records in 1953, with the Parrot label in Chicago, and moved frequently, working regularly in and around Osceola and traveling to Chicago and St. Louis for gigs and recording dates. From 1966 through 1969 he had several hits—"Laundromat Blues," "Crosscut Saw," "Born under a Bad Sign"—as the only blues act on Stax/Volt's legendary soul label. Soon he was playing bigger venues—in 1968 alone he appeared at San Francisco's Winterland and Fillmore East, Chicago's Regal Theater, and New York's Carnegie Hall. *Born under a Bad Sign* (1967) was one of the top blues albums of the decade.

By this time King was an international star—he toured England with his own band in 1968 and played the famed Montreux festivals in Switzerland twice (in 1973 and 1975). King was a major influence on younger musicians, from blues-centered stars like Luther Allison, Son Seals, Otis Rush, and Johnny Winter to rockers like Jimi Hendrix, Eric Clapton, and Robbie Robertson. King died in 1992.

Tracy Lawrence

Tracy Lawrence was born in Texas in 1968, and raised in Foreman, Arkansas. His mother hoped for a ministerial calling, but her son was drawn to music early—he wrote his first song at four and was singing in local bands by the time he was sixteen. In 1986 he enrolled at Southern

Arkansas University in Magnolia, but left after two years to front a Louisiana band. His models were Merle Haggard, Keith Whitley, Waylon Jennings, and (most of all) George Strait.

Moving to Nashville "in a ten-year-old Toyota Corolla with about 250,000 miles on it" in 1990, Lawrence worked various day jobs, entered talent contests, and waited for his break. It came in 1991, when he signed with Atlantic and recorded *Sticks and Stones,* his debut album. The single of the same title was a #1 hit—the first country hit to grab the top spot for Atlantic. From the beginning, however, Lawrence's silver star rose with a clouded lining. Even before the album's release, he was shot four times in a robbery attempt outside his Nashville hotel. Then, after *Billboard* tabbed him "Best New Male Artist" in 1992, and the Academy of Country Music named him "Top New Male Vocalist" in 1993, Lawrence grabbed bad headlines again in 1994 when law officers in Wilson County, Tennessee, charged him with reckless endangerment for squeezing off a few rounds in a dispute with local teenagers.

FIGURE 56 Tracy Lawrence, 2002. *Reproduced by permission of Getty Images*

Other hits and additional misadventures followed. In 1993 his second album, *Alibis,* went platinum shortly after its release and generated three consecutive #1 singles ("Alibis," "Can't Break It to My Heart," and "My Second Home"). Two other well-received efforts followed—*Time Marches On* in 1996, and *The Coast Is Clear* in 1997. In 1998, however, there were additional brushes with the law, with the troubled star up before the judge on a spousal abuse charge.

In country music, however, you can't keep a bad boy down. Lawrence was soon back with *Lessons Learned* in 2000 and *Tracy Lawrence* in 2001. Maybe the former is even accurately titled—recent headlines have been positive notices of concerts for the troops in Kosovo and hometown benefits endowing scholarships and equipping his old high school's computer science lab.

Roberta Martin

Roberta Evelyn Winston was born February 12, 1907, in Helena. At ten she moved with her family to Illinois, settling in Chicago, but long before this her precocious musical talent had been recognized when she climbed up on piano benches and picked out melodies she'd heard. Her brother's wife was her first piano teacher.

FIGURE 57 Roberta Martin. *Courtesy of Tulane University Library*

Graduating from Wendell Phillips High School, Winston changed her name to Martin and began serving as Sunday School pianist for Pilgrim Baptist Church. In 1932 she became pianist for the junior choir at Ebenezer Baptist Church, and by 1935 she had organized her first gospel group, the Martin-Frye Quartet (this group became the Roberta Martin Singers in 1936). By the 1940s Martin had mixed male and female voices to create one of gospel music's best-known and most-enduring groups, with a widely admired and much-imitated "refined" form of Pentecostal gospel tradition. Many famous vocalists—Robert Anderson, Delois Barrett Campbell, James Cleveland, Archie Davis, Norsalus McKissick, Della Reese, Eugene Smith, and Dinah Washington, among others—either got their start or rose to fame as members of her groups.

Martin also achieved fame as a gospel songwriter and publisher. One of her first publications (in 1939) was "He Knows How Much We Can Bear," a number that is sometimes mistakenly credited as her composition. Her first success as a writer was "Try Jesus, He Satisfies" in 1943. Martin subsequently wrote several other songs that have become standards—"God Is

Still on the Throne" (1959) and "I'm Just Waiting On the Lord" (1953) are two examples. She published songs by other composers as well, including Alex Bradford, James Cleveland, and Dorothy Norwood.

When Martin died in 1969, tens of thousands of admirers attended her memorial service. In 1981 she was honored by the Smithsonian Institution.

Patsy Montana

Born near Hot Springs (in the now-disappeared Beaudry settlement) in 1908, Rubye Blevins became Patsy Montana in the early 1930s, in California, when she became one of three "Montana Cowgirls" in a troupe headed by Stuart Hamblen and cowboy star Monte Montana. Back in Arkansas she appeared on nearby KWKH in Shreveport, Louisiana, where RCA Victor star Jimmie Davis heard her and used her to play fiddle and sing backup on his records. But big fame didn't come until 1935 when her own composition, "I Want to Be a Cowboy's Sweetheart," recorded with the Prairie Ramblers and featuring Montana's superb yodeling, became the first million-selling hit by a female country singer.

A long and busy career followed—fifteen years of touring with the Prairie Ramblers, twenty-five years as a regular on the WLS Barn Dance, several other hit songs, including "I'm an Old Cowhand" (1937) and "Singing in the Saddle" (1938), and at least one role in a feature film (*Colorado Sunset,* 1940). In 1946–1947 she had her own network radio show on ABC, "Wake Up and Smile." Between 1934 and 1992, Montana made over seven thousand personal appearances in the United States, Canada, and

FIGURE 58 Patsy Montana. *Courtesy of Old State House Museum Collections, Little Rock*

Europe. In August 1995, just two months before her eighty-first birthday, she returned for a concert in Hope, where she graduated from high school in 1932. Among the several "sweetheart" songs she recorded in the wake of her big hit were "I Only Want a Buddy not a Sweetheart" and "Little Sweetheart of the Ozarks." Montana died in 1996.

K. T. Oslin

FIGURE 59 K. T. Oslin. *Reproduced by permission of Getty Images*

Kay Toinette Oslin was born in Crossett in 1942. After her father died when she was five, Kay and her brother were raised by their mother in Alabama and Texas. While her mother sang swing tunes on local radio, Kay's tastes ran to country music as a youngster, then to folk music in college. She formed a Houston folk trio in 1962 with radio producer Chuck Jones and songwriter Guy Clark.

She later formed a folk duo with Frank Davis in Hollywood, but their album was never released. Oslin then put her drama degree to use, joining the road company of *Hello Dolly!* After the tour ended in 1966, she had small roles in other musicals and sang jingles while she began writing songs and trying to get noticed in Nashville. In 1987, Oslin made her debut on RCA with a remake of Gus Hardin's "Wall of Tears," which became a modest radio hit. Then, when she was forty-five, Oslin's own "80's Ladies," her second RCA effort, struck a chord nationwide, selling a million copies and winning a Grammy. She also had #1 hits with "Do Ya" and "Hold Me." In 1988 Oslin became the first female songwriter to win Song of the Year from the Country Music Association. She also took first place as Female Vocalist of the Year.

To writer Holly Gleason she emphasized her desire to write her songs from a woman's perspective: "While there've always been women singers in country music, they've always been singing songs written by men that reflect the way men think women feel. Now you find that people are finally saying, 'Hey, the women songwriters have something to say.' The songs are truly from a woman's point of view."

Point of Grace

Shelley Breen, Denise Jones, Terry Jones, and Heather Payne first sang together as students at Ouachita Baptist University in 1991. A decade later they're one of the most successful groups in the gospel music business, with eight albums to their credit. *Point of Grace,* in 1993, was their first; *Girls of Grace* (which includes performances by other female Christian acts), in 2002, is their most recent; and *Life, Love and Other*

FIGURE 60 Point of Grace.
Courtesy of Shelley Breen

Mysteries, from 1996, is their top seller. They've garnered fourteen Dove Awards, two Grammy nominations, and a lengthy string of consecutive #1 singles (twenty-four at one recent count).

All this points to the wide appeal of Point of Grace among gospel fans, but the group has in recent years staked out an especially strong niche among teenage girls. Concerts include birthday and pregnancy announcements, testimonials on the importance of premarital abstinence, and plugs for the Nashville-centered Mercy Ministries of America. The group's website provides the birthday of each member along with year of marriage, names of husbands, children, and dogs. (Birth *years,* however, are omitted, as in all of Twila Paris's publicity; it's unclear why gospel divas, stressing as they do the ephemerality of secular attachments, should be so much more reluctant than singers in other genres to divulge their worldly ages.)

Charlie Rich

Born in Colt in 1932, Charlie Rich grew up surrounded by the whole panorama of southern music, from the white gospel music he heard with his parents at church, to the country music they listened to on the *Grand Ole Opry,* to the blues piano he learned from a black sharecropper named C. J. on his father's farm. He learned it all, but found jazz especially attractive, often citing Stan Kenton, Billie Holiday, and George Gershwin as particular favorites.

After a year at the University of Arkansas and a stint in the U.S. Air Force, Rich was hired as a session player by Bill Justis at Sun Records in Memphis, where he played local bars, wrote songs with his wife, Margaret Ann, and in 1960 had his first big hit with "Lonely Weekends." In 1965 he had another smash, "Mohair Sam," on Mercury, and in 1973, on Epic, "Behind Closed Doors" became his first #1 hit and gold record. The followup, "The Most Beautiful Girl," did even better, going platinum by passing the two-million sales mark and helping him win a Grammy and the Country Music Association's Male Vocalist of the Year Award.

Such early seventies triumphs were the high-water mark for the man who by then was called "the Silver Fox." Troubles followed, caused at times by drinking and at times by excessive honesty. At the 1975 CMA awards show, on national television, he opened the envelope for Entertainer of the Year (won by Rich himself in 1974), saw that John Denver had won, whipped out his lighter, and set the offending document ablaze.

But if the CMA incident reveals his panache, a deeper look at Rich is provided by Greil Marcus's memory of his appearance at an industry party sponsored by Columbia Records in 1973. Rich closed the show, following a procession of artists there to entertain the businessmen who allowed them to make money, and because he "was the star of the day, the men running the show gave him an encore." He played "Feel Like Going Home," a double-edged choice in itself, given the scene, but before he played he gave the song a dedicatory introduction: "Today," Rich said, "I would like to dedicate this song to the President of the United States.'"

FIGURE 61 Charlie Rich. *Reproduced by permission of Getty Images*

That was Richard Nixon, of course, just then going over the edge in the Watergate debacle, his "whole existence . . . a national joke." But Rich wasn't playing for cheap laughs, and when he sang the lonely song's aching lyrics, "I tried and I failed / And I feel like going home," he hit Marcus hard: "They cut through everything I believe to uncover a compassion that I never, never wanted to feel."

Rich, all this says, was at once a troubled man and a very great artist. He could bring enlargement, even if he was often trapped himself, sitting in places where he didn't want to be, singing and playing songs he didn't want to sing. Rich died in 1995.

Almeda Riddle

Almeda James was born in 1898 in Cleburne County. She learned ballads and other traditional songs from her mother and her maternal uncle John Wilkerson, but it was her father, J. L. James, a timber worker, singing teacher, and fiddler, who most encouraged her interest in music. In 1916 she married H. P. Riddle, who shared her love of singing, but ten years later, in 1926, her husband and infant son were killed in a cyclone in Heber Springs, leaving her with three young children to raise.

FIGURE 62 Almeda Riddle.
Courtesy of Andrew Kilgore

Riddle collected songs all her life—"I knew my notes before I knew my letters," she said—but it wasn't until about 1950, after her children were married, that she was able to work more steadily on her "book of ballads." Before the decade was out she'd been "discovered" by folklorist John Quincy Wolf when a neighbor answered his newspaper ad in search of traditional singers, and she spent the rest of her life making records and appearing at colleges and folk festivals throughout the nation.

During this period she appeared in concert and on records with most of the best-known figures of the "folk revival" period, including Pete Seeger and the New Lost City Ramblers. In 1966 Riddle represented Arkansas at the National Festival of American Folklife in Washington, D.C., and in 1971 her life and music were the subject of a book-length study, *A Singer and Her Songs,* edited by folklorist Roger Abrahams. Riddle died in 1986.

Billy Lee Riley

Billy Riley was born October 5, 1933, in Pocahontas, and grew up on various Arkansas and Mississippi farms. His father taught him harmonica and he picked up the guitar from neighbors. Mustered out of the army in 1954—he'd lied about his age to enlist in 1949—Riley moved to Memphis, joined Slim Wallace's Dixie Ramblers, and in 1956 opened a productive and tumultuous relationship with Sam Phillips's Sun Records. Riley's biggest successes were "Flying Saucer Rock and Roll" and "Red Hot," both from 1957 (though the former was recorded in 1956). Riley and Phillips clashed (sometimes violently) over promotion—Phillips pushed Jerry Lee Lewis's "Great Balls of Fire" over Riley's "Red Hot."

FIGURE 63 Billy Lee Riley. *Courtesy of Sun Entertainment Corporation*

Riley's early disappointments continue to rankle—Phillips gets a grilling at every opportunity, but his career has flourished in recent years. He's been filmed for a Smithsonian documentary and opened for Bob Dylan. Riley continues to perform steadily (in Europe and in the United States) and also to record; in 1992 he released *Blue Collar Blues,* and in 1997 his *Hot Damn!* was nominated for a Grammy. *Shade Tree Blues* followed in 1999, and Riley's latest is the 2002 *One More Time.* On all of these, the rockabilly frenzy of the early Sun cuts is matched by convincing blues and R&B performances.

Son Seals

Frank Junior Seals was born in Osceola in 1942, where his father Jim Seals, a musician who had toured with the Rabbit Foot Minstrels, owned the Dipsy Doodle Club. Seals started as a

FIGURE 64 Son Seals.
Courtesy of Robert Cochran

drummer, working in his father's club with such greats as Sonny Boy Williamson, Robert Nighthawk, and fellow Osceola resident Albert King. About 1959 he learned guitar and formed his own band, the Upsetters, to work the local T99 Club and the Chez Paris in Little Rock. In the 1960s he toured as a drummer and rhythm guitarist with Earl Hooker's Roadmasters and with Albert King, playing the Fillmore in San Francisco with King and appearing on his *Live Wire/Blues Power* album.

In 1971 Seals moved to Chicago after his father's death, where he played with Hound Dog Taylor before forming his own group to play the Expressway Lounge in 1972. His first album, *The Son Seals Blues Band,* was released on the new Chicago label Alligator in 1973, followed by *Midnight Son* in 1974, and *Live and Burning* in 1978. By 1977 he had been to Europe, appearing in London with B. B. King and playing the Nancy Jazz Festival in France. Seals still lives in Chicago, where he finds steady work in clubs when he's not on tour, but his Arkansas roots remain strong. "I tell you, man, I'd go back there today if I could just make it economically," he told writer Peter Guralnick. "People down home really knew how to enjoy themselves. Every Sunday is the fourth of July."

Johnnie Taylor

Johnnie Taylor was born in Crawfordsville, May 5, 1938. He grew up mostly in West Memphis, and had his first record in 1955 as a member of a doo-wop called the Five Echoes. In the same year he sang lead on the

Highway QCs gospel hit, "Somewhere to Lay My Head," and in 1957 he moved into big shoes, replacing Sam Cooke as the Soul Stirrers' lead. After a brief stint on Cooke's SAR label, Taylor signed with Stax in 1965, and proved himself a potent soul artist, producing "I Had a Dream," "I've Got to Love Somebody's Baby," and especially "Who's Making Love" (though the little-known "Next Time," from 1968, is just as powerful as the bigger hits).

Following the demise of Stax, Taylor recorded with several labels before landing with Malaco in 1984. His biggest hit, however, was the 1976 "Disco Lady" (the first-ever platinum single) on Columbia. Doo-wop, gospel, soul, disco—Taylor could and did it all. And Malaco let him do it, from first (*This Is Your Night* in 1984) to last (*Good Love!* in 1996). Taylor was a magnificent singer, equally capable of Sam Cooke's smooth clarity and Wilson Pickett's throaty rasp. He was a big star, but listening to his music makes you wonder why he wasn't even bigger. Taylor died in 2000.

FIGURE 65 Johnny Taylor. *Courtesy of Geleve Grice*

Rosetta Tharpe

Rosetta Nubin was born in 1921 in Cotton Plant. She was influenced in both her religious views and her musical interests by her mother, Katie Bell Nubin, "Mother Bell," a traveling Holiness Church evangelist. By the age of six Tharpe was touring professionally as a vocalist and guitarist, doing both gospel and secular performances. In 1938, the year of her first recordings, she performed (along with fellow Arkansas native Bill Broonzy) at John Hammond's famous "Spirituals to Swing" concert at Carnegie Hall, and in 1939, after appearing at the Cotton Club with Cab Calloway, she became the first gospel artist to record for a major label when she signed with Decca Records. In a lengthy career that lasted from the 1940s into the 1960s, Tharpe sang everywhere, sometimes

FIGURE 66 Rosetta Tharpe.
Reproduced by permission of
Getty Images

offending the faithful by singing in nightclubs just as she surprised the Saturday night crowds with her devotion to the values of Sunday morning. The result was a new, hybrid music—she "invented pop gospel," wrote one admiring critic.

Few artists covered such a range of styles—performing with blues musicians (Muddy Waters), jazz artists (Calloway and Lucky Millinder), and other gospel groups (the Caravans, the Dixie Hummingbirds, the James Cleveland Singers). Few appeared in so many places either—from the early Carnegie Hall and Cotton Club gigs to the Apollo Theatre in 1943 (and 1960), to the Newport Folk Festival in 1967, to European tours in the 1950s and 1960s. And certainly no performer in any style matched Sister Tharpe's talent for self-dramatization —as demonstrated perhaps most spectacularly in her 1951 marriage, number three, to her manager, Russell Morrison. The ceremony took place in Washington, D.C.'s Griffith Stadium, where a crowd of twenty-five thousand witnessed the ceremony, heard a concert, and was treated to a fireworks display featuring an enormous portrait of the star herself, wielding a guitar. Decca recorded, and later released, the whole show.

Tharpe's biggest hits were "This Train" (1938), with her own guitar accompaniment, "Strange Things Happening Every Day" (1944, with boogie-woogie pianist Sammy Price), and "Up Above My Head" (1946, with Marie Knight). Tharpe died in Philadelphia in 1973.

Conway Twitty

Conway Twitty was born Harold Lloyd Jenkins on September 1, 1933, in Friar's Point, Mississippi, and raised mostly in Helena, where he attended high school. His grandfather taught him guitar, and he was performing on KFFA by the time he was twelve. Soon enough he was a regular, appearing on Sunday mornings with two high school pals as the Phillips County Ramblers.

Jenkins also played baseball well enough to be scouted by the Philadelphia Phillies. He was drafted in to the army during the Korean War, and when he got out in 1956 he recorded eight unissued songs for Sun

FIGURE 67 Conway Twitty with Loretta Lynn, 1972. *Reproduced by permission of Getty Images*

before signing with Mercury as a rockabilly act and making a new name for himself by yoking an Arkansas town (Conway) to a Texas one (Twitty). In 1958 he struck paydirt; having signed with MGM, he recorded "It's Only Make Believe" and rode it to the #1 spot. Other chart toppers followed in quick succession ("Danny Boy" in 1959, "What Am I Living For" in 1960), and soon Twitty was appearing in teen movies as well.

Sensing the end of the rockabilly ride, Twitty remodeled himself as a country artist in 1965, and by 1968 he'd made it to #1 again with "Next in Line." Working alone and in tandem with Loretta Lynn, he produced a long string of hits in the 1970s and 1980s. He was also an active businessman; Twitty Enterprises produced Twitty burgers and Conway Twitty Mobile Homes and owned the Nashville Sounds minor league baseball team, among other ventures. Twitty died in 1993.

FIGURE 68 Lucinda Williams. *Courtesy of Richard Berquist*

Lucinda Williams

Lucinda Williams was born in Lake Charles, Louisiana, in 1953, and lived in Macon, Georgia; Jackson, Mississippi; and Baton Rouge, Louisiana, before moving to Fayetteville in 1971. She was twelve when she gave her first public performance for a Baton Rouge PTA meeting in 1965, and by the early 1970s she was performing regularly in clubs and coffeehouses in Arkansas and Texas.

Williams cut her first album, *Ramblin' on My Mind,* in 1979, for Folkways. It was heavy on traditional blues and country numbers (three Robert Johnson songs, plus renditions of Hank Williams's "Jambalaya" and the Carter Family's "Little Darling Pal of Mine"). Her next effort, the *Happy Woman Blues* of 1980, also on Folkways, included several of her own songs.

Williams moved to Los Angeles in 1984, and in 1988 her third album, *Lucinda Williams,* was made up almost entirely of original material (a version of Howlin' Wolf's "Asked Her for Water [She

Gave Me Gasoline]" is the only cut not written by Williams). Other singers began recording her songs; Mary Chapin-Carpenter did "Passionate Kisses" and Patty Loveless recorded "The Night's Too Long." In 1992 Williams released two albums, *Passionate Kisses* and *Sweet Old World*. *Car Wheels on a Gravel Road* followed in 1998, with *Essence* appearing in 2001, and *World without Tears* in 2003.

Sonny Boy Williamson

He went to great lengths to mislead and confuse would-be biographers, but his real name was Aleck Miller—he was the son of Millie Ford but took his name from his stepfather, Jim Miller—and he was probably born in Glendora, Mississippi, in 1899 (though dates as early as 1894 and as late as 1910 have been suggested). Miller was a self-taught harmonica

FIGURE 69 Sonny Boy Williamson. *Reproduced by permission of Getty Images*

prodigy who was playing for local parties by the age of six or seven. He spent most of his life as an itinerant musician, working Arkansas and Mississippi juke joints, clubs, lumber camps, and street corners while occasionally ranging as far as New Orleans and Nashville, where he is said to have played on the *Grand Ole Opry* in the 1930s.

Miller made his first records with the Jackson, Mississippi, Trumpet label in 1951, but long before this—since 1941—he'd been calling himself Sonny Boy Williamson on the now-famous radio blues show, "King Biscuit Time," carried by KFFA in Helena. In 1954 his recording contract was purchased by the Chess label in Chicago, and his several subsequent hits ("One Way Out," "99," "Fattening Frogs for Snakes," "Your Funeral and My Trial") were followed by successful European tours in 1963 and 1964. Like Big Bill Broonzy before him, Miller enjoyed the appreciation of European fans. He considered moving to

England, where he appeared in concerts with the Animals and the Yardbirds, but he eventually returned to Helena where he appeared again on the "King Biscuit Show" in 1965, the year of his death.

Among his less-noted pieces is a fine song he called "Wake Up, Baby," which is in fact a version of the old Scottish ballad most commonly known as "Our Goodman" in folk-song collections. It's found in David Herd's *Ancient and Modern Scottish Songs,* published in 1776, and it's a Child ballad (#274), just like those so prized by collectors when old ladies or gentlemen in the Ozarks or Ouachitas sing them. But here it has mostly escaped notice, appearing as it did on a pop rhythm and blues album produced in Chicago and featuring a black harmonica player. All these white boys, Levon Helm and Robbie Robertson and Eric Clapton and Eric Burdon, getting so much from Sonny Boy, it's good to know he took something back from their grandmas.

NOTES

1 ✿ With Fiddles and Hymnals

1. Nicolas de La Salle, quoted in George Sabo, "Rituals of Encounter: Interpreting Native American Views of European Explorers," in Jeannie Whayne, ed., *Cultural Encounters in the Early South: Indians and Europeans in Arkansas* (Fayetteville: University of Arkansas Press, 1995), 77. For the cane flute and whistle, see Mark R. Harrington, *The Ozark Bluff-Dwellers* (New York: Museum of the American Indian/Heye Foundation, 1971 [first published 1960]), 162, and plates XXXVd, XXXVId. For the Quapaw robe, see *Robes of Splendor: Native American Painted Buffalo Hides* (New York: New Press, 1993), 137. There is a color close-up of the dancer carrying a rattle on page 56. The robe is discussed in penetrating detail in Morris S. Arnold, "Eighteenth-Century Arkansas Illustrated," *Arkansas Historical Quarterly* 53 (1994): 119–36. As Arnold notes, the skin may not in fact be a robe; a partition, a tablecloth, and a bedspread have been suggested. There is a black and white close-up of the dancer carrying a rattle on page 124, and Arnold's note 29 (127) includes a thorough catalogue of references to Quapaw music and instruments. For a superb summary of the DeSoto entrada and its many investigators, see David Sloan, "The Expedition of Hernando DeSoto: A Post-mortem Report," in Whayne, ed., *Cultural Encounters,* 3–37.

2. Henri Joutel, *The Last Voyage Perform'd by de la Sale* (Ann Arbor, MI: University Microfilms, 1966 [reprint of 1714 English edition], 146–47.

3. John Francis McDermott, ed., *Tixier's "Travels on the Osage Prairies"* (Norman: University of Oklahoma Press, 1940 [translation of 1844 French edition]), 239.

4. James F. Keefe and Lynn Morrow, eds., *The White River Chronicles of S. C. Turnbo* (Fayetteville: University of Arkansas Press, 1994), 7.

5. François Marie Perrin du Lac, *Voyage dans les Deux Louisianes . . . en 1801, 1802, et 1803* (Lyons, 1805), 360 (cited by Morris S. Arnold, "The Significance of Arkansas's Colonial Experience," in Whayne, ed., *Cultural Encounters,* 138).

6. Morris S. Arnold, *Colonial Arkansas, 1686–1804: A Social and Cultural Hisstory* (Fayetteville: University of Arkansas Press, 1991), 71.

7. Savoie Lottinville, ed., *A Journal of Travels into the Arkansas Territory During the Year 1819, By Thomas Nuttall* (Norman: University of Oklahoma Press, 1980), 88.

8. George W. Featherstonhaugh, *Excursion Through the Slave States* (London: John Murray, 1844), vol. II, 177.

9. Friedrich Gerstäcker, *Wild Sports in the Far West* (Durham, NC: Duke University Press, 1968), 142, 220, 223, 224. For similar accounts of other early "frolics," see John Quincy Wolf, *Life in the Leatherwoods* (Little Rock, AR: August House, 1988 [first published 1974]), 132–34. This is an account of an Izard County square dance in the 1870s. See also Leonard Williams, "An Early Arkansas 'Frolic': A Contemporary Account," *Mid-South Folklore* 2 (1974): 39–42, for a reprinting of a Charles F. Noland ("Pete Whetstone") piece first published in 1837.

10. Featherstonhaugh, *Excursion Through the Slave States,* 210–11.

11. Thomas Bangs Thorpe, "The Big Bear of Arkansas," in Walter Blair, ed., *Native American Humor* (Scranton, PA: Chandler, 1960 [first published in 1841]), 337; Herman Melville, *Moby-Dick* (Evanston and Chicago: Northwestern University Press and The Newberry Library, 1988 [first published in 1851]), 184; Frederick Marryat, *The Travels and Adventures of Monsieur Violet in California, Sonora, and Western Texas* (London, 1858), 285; quoted in James Masterson, *Arkansas Folklore* (Little Rock, AR: Rose, 1974), 4.

12. Masterson, *Arkansas Folklore,* 186.

13. For detailed information on "The Arkansas Traveler," see Masterson, *Arkansas Folklore,* chapters 14 through 17, 186–254. I have seen Len Spencer's name spelled "Spenser," but W. K. McNeil tells me Spencer is correct. For good discussions of visual treatments of the story, see the articles by Sarah Brown, Archie Green, and George Lankford cited in the bibliography.

14. "The State of Arkansaw" was first printed in John A. Lomax's *Cowboy Songs and Other Frontier Ballads* (New York: Sturgis and Walton, 1910), though it was probably circulating orally in the 1890s. James Masterson's *Arkansas Folklore* devotes chapter 18 ("A Hobo in Arkansaw") to the song, and Vance Randolph prints six versions (one by Emma Dusenbury) in *Ozark Folksongs* (Columbia, University of Missouri Press, 1980), vol. III, 25–33.

15. For two fragmentary versions of "Down in Arkansas," see Randolph, *Ozark Folksongs,* vol. III, 34–35. For three versions of "The Arkansas Boys," see the same volume, 12–14, and more especially W. K. McNeil, ed., *Southern Mountain Folksongs* (Little Rock, AR: August House, 1993), 186–88, 234–35. As "The Arkansas Sheik," it was recorded by Clayton McMichen and Riley Puckett for Columbia in 1928. A modern version of "Down in the Arkansas" is on record in the 1972 National Geographic recording *Music of the Ozarks*—for lyrics see Leo Rainey, *Songs of the Ozark Folk* (Branson, MO: Ozarks Mountaineer, 1976), 16–17. For biographical sketches of Evans, see the reference works by Claghorn, Gammond, and Kinkle cited in the bibliography. Evans, who was born in Wales in 1870, is mistakenly described in some sources as being African American.

16. Featherstonhaugh, *Excursion Through the Slave States,* 194, 202–3, 205.

17. Ruth Polk Patterson, *The Seed of Sally Good'n: A Black Family of Arkansas, 1833–1953* (Lexington: University Press of Kentucky, 1980), 98–99. "Sally Goodin" is described as "popular at play-parties in the early 90's" [that's 1890s] by Randolph (*Ozark Folksongs,* vol. III, 350) and as "one of the most popular fiddle tunes on record, with well over fifty recordings by traditional southern musicians" by Norm Cohen, ed., *Ozark Folksongs* (Urbana: University of Illinois Press, 1982 [revised and abridged edition]), 403. We'll see it again as a famous country music record with ties to Arkansas.

18. George P. Rawick, ed., *The American Slave: A Composite Autobiography* (Westport, CT: Greenwood, 1972), suppl., ser. 2, vol. 1, i.

19. Rawick, *The American Slave,* vol. 10, pt. 5, 285.

20. Rawick, *The American Slave,* vol. 8, pt. 1, 18.

21. Rawick, *The American Slave,* suppl., ser. 2, vol. 1, 60.

22. Rawick, *The American Slave,* suppl., ser. 2, vol. 1, 88–89.

23. Rawick, *The American Slave,* vol. 8, pt. 1, 254.

24. Rawick, *The American Slave,* vol. 8, pt. 2, 116, 109.

25. Rawick, *The American Slave,* vol. 10, pt. 6, 131–32.

26. Rawick, *The American Slave,* vol. 8, pt. 1, 11.

27. Rawick, *The American Slave,* vol. 8, pt. 1, 35.

28. Rawick, *The American Slave,* vol. 8, pt. 1, 64.

29. Rawick, *The American Slave,* vol. 8, pt. 1, 236. The quoted stanzas are from two separate songs, the first commonly known as "The Homespun Dress" and the second as either "The Pea Ridge Battle" or "General Price." See Randolph, *Ozark Folksongs,* vol. II, 262–63, 247–50.

30. Rawick, *The American Slave,* vol. 8, pt. 2, 27.

31. Rawick, *The American Slave,* vol. 8, pt. 1, 247.

32. A copy of Miller's song is in the permanent collection of the Old State House Museum; on it Miller is identified as the son of a New Jersey senator, and the song is reported as having been published in a volume titled *Black Soldiers, Black Sailors, Black Ink.*

33. Ted R. Worley, ed., *They Never Came Back: The War Memoirs of Captain John W. Lavender, C.S.A.* (Pine Bluff, AR: W. M. Hackett and D. R. Perdue, c. 1956), 5, 126–27.

34. Daniel E. Sutherland, ed., *Reminiscences of a Private: William E. Bevens of the First Arkansas Infantry, C.S.A.* (Fayetteville: University of Arkansas Press, 1992), 37. A vivid anecdote not specific to Arkansas illustrates the importance of music in the life of soldiers: "Rival armies were camped within earshot of one another the night before the Battle of Murfreesboro. At one point the Northern band played 'Yankee Doodle,' and the Southern band responded with a patriotic Rebel tune; the two bands alternated this way for some time, then they played 'Home, Sweet Home' together. The next morning the armies slaughtered one another by the thousands." Charles Hamm, *Yesterdays: Popular Song in America* (New York: Norton, 1979), 231.

35. Randolph, *Ozark Folksongs,* vol. II, 246.

36. Randolph, *Ozark Folksongs,* vol. II, 261, 294. Harry Macarthy (or MacCarthy) was born in England in 1834, and wrote "The Bonnie Blue Flag" in Mississippi in 1861. His sobriquet seems to be his only connection with Arkansas. "Dixie" itself originated outside the South—it was written by Ohio native Dan Emmett in 1859—but many verses by various hands and of widely varying sentiments were soon in circulation. See Michael P. Dougan, *Confederate Arkansas: The People and Politics of a Frontier State in Wartime* (Tuscaloosa: University of Alabama Press, 1976), 58–59.

37. Work was a native of Connecticut who wrote several well-known war songs, including "Marching through Georgia." "The Year of Jubelo" is more commonly known as "Kingdom Coming," and was first published in 1862. The lovely first line of the last stanza, "The whip is lost an' the handcuff's busted," may be echoed a century later in The Band's "We Can Talk About It Now," written by Richard Manuel—"No need to slave, / The whip is in the grave."

38. Roger D. Abrahams, ed., *A Singer and Her Songs: Almeda Riddle's Book of Ballads* (Baton Rouge: Louisiana State University Press, 1970), 13.

39. Cited in Sheldon Harris, *Blues Who's Who* (New Rochelle, NY: Arklington House, c. 1979), 559. Information on Essie Whitman and the Whitman Sisters also comes from Ross Russell, *Jazz Style in Kansas City and the Southwest* (Berkeley: University of California Press, 1971), 13, 81, 219.

40. Christopher S. Wren, *Winners Got Scars Too: The Life and Legends of Johnny Cash* (New York: Dial, 1971), 34.

2 ✿ Radios and Phonographs

1. Ray Poindexter, *Arkansas Airwaves* (North Little Rock, AR: no publisher listed, 1974), 7. Poindexter's book lacks an index, and its organization is haphazard throughout, but it is nevertheless a mine of information about the early days of radio in Arkansas.

Poindexter, himself an Arkansan, worked in radio all over the state—starting at KBTM in Jonesboro, he soon moved on to KELD in El Dorado, KDRS in Paragould, KNBY in Newport, and KVLC in Little Rock. His account, though impersonal in the main, is enlivened at several points by his own reminiscences. There is in fact a direct connection between the early research at the University of Arkansas and the first station at Pine Bluff. The honor of selecting the WOK call letters was given to Arkansas Light and Power vice president J. C. Longino, who as a student at the university in 1897–1898 had worked on wireless telegraphy with engineering professor W. N. Gladson.

2. Poindexter, *Arkansas Airwaves,* 17–18.

3. Poindexter, *Arkansas Airwaves,* 28.

4. Poindexter, *Arkansas Airwaves,* 52.

5. Poindexter, *Arkansas Airwaves,* 90, 91–92, 93.

6. Poindexter, *Arkansas Airwaves,* 114, 105.

7. Poindexter, *Arkansas Airwaves,* 249, 257.

8. Poindexter, *Arkansas Airwaves,* 142, 145, 146. Somehow one doubts that Miss Todd's rendition of "Ding Dong Daddy from Dumas" was identical to the version recorded in 1937 by Texas Playboys vocalist Tommy Duncan—the "Daddy" in this instance being a pusher offering to "sell you morphine, coke, or snow." Surely this fellow hailed from the Texas Dumas.

9. Robert Palmer, *Deep Blues: A Musical and Cultural History of the Mississippi Delta* (New York: Penguin, 1981), 185–86. Palmer's survey, unlike many blues histories, gives due attention to Arkansas music, recognizing that the Mississippi River is not (and was not) a major cultural divide. It had two sides, there were bridges and ferries across it, and musicians used them frequently. Palmer was a native of Little Rock.

10. Peter Guralnick, *Searching for Robert Johnson* (New York: E. P. Dutton, 1989), 28.

11. Palmer, *Deep Blues,* 178.

12. Kenneth S. Goldstein, "The Impact of Recording Technology on the British Folksong Revival," in William Ferris and Mary L. Hart, eds., *Folk Music and Modern Sound* (Jackson: University Press of Mississippi, 1982), 4.

13. For a detailed discussion of Smith's recording and the early blues recording milieu generally, see Jeff Todd Titon, *Early Downhome Blues* (Urbana: University of Illinois Press, 1977); chapter 6, pages 197–224, is titled "Recording the Blues." Smith's recording of "Crazy Blues" is discussed on page 204. The Campbell/Gilliland recording was not released until 1923. For a comparable discussion of pioneer country music recordings, see Bill C. Malone, *Country Music U.S.A.* (Austin: University of Texas Press, 1985 [first published 1968]); chapter 2, pages 31–75, is titled "The Early Period of

Commercial Hillbilly Music." The Campbell/Gilliland session is discussed on page 35.

14. Don Cusic, *The Sound of Light: A History of Gospel Music* (Bowling Green, Ohio: Bowling Green State University Press, 1990), 73.

15. Russell, *Jazz Style in Kansas City and the Southwest,* 61. Trent's music can be heard on *Territory Bands 1929–33* (Historical HLP-24). For a detailed portrait of Trent and his band, see Henry Q. Rinne, "A Short History of the Alphonso Trent Orchestra," *Arkansas Historical Quarterly* 45 (1986): 228–49.

16. Harris, *Blues Who's Who,* 547, credits the marriage, but it is called into question by Paul and Beth Garon in *Woman with Guitar: Memphis Minnie's Blues* (New York: Da Capo Press, 1992), 20–21, 287.

17. Information on early Arkansas string bands comes from the liner notes by Dave Freeman for the two-CD *Echoes of the Ozarks* collection on the County label, and especially from W. K. McNeil, "Five Pre–World War II Arkansas String Bands: Some Thoughts on Their Recording Success," *John Edwards Memorial Foundation Quarterly* 20 (1984): 68–75. The observation that the organ is "an instrument much more common in Southern old time dance music than its relatively rare appearance on commercial recordings might indicate" comes from this article (70). I have seen a reference (in Nick Tosches, *Country: The Biggest Music in America,* 210) to a 1927 recording by Reaves White County Ramblers, but my guess is that McNeil's dates are correct. McNeil's knowledge of the state's folk, blues, country, and gospel music is encyclopedic, and his fieldwork as a collector of both music and traditional narrative makes him Vance Randolph's true successor as the leading student of Ozark traditional culture. I have benefited enormously from his generous aid in this and in other projects.

18. For additional information on the Horse-Hair Pullers, see Helen C. Lindley, "The Hoss-Hair Pullers and Hillbilly Quartet," *Izard County Historian* 5 (1974): 9–13.

19. Apsie Morrison was recorded again in 1959 by Alan Lomax and Shirley Collins, with three selections released on *Ballads and Breakdowns from the Southern Mountains* (Prestige International INT-DS 25003), which has "The Scotch Music," and *Folk Songs from the Ozarks* (Prestige International INT- DS 25006), which has "My Pretty Little Girl Is Gone" and "Nancy's Got a Purty Dress On." For a very interesting article on the historical commentaries Morrison provided for his tunes, see Judith McCulloh, "Uncle Absie Morrison's Historical Tunes," *Mid-South Folklore* 3 (1975): 95–104. "Absie" and "Apsie" are the same man—such variations were common when writing was uncommon. Emma Dusenbury's surname has been spelled at least three ways in print.

20. Charley Patton's lyrics are notoriously unintelligible—for two guesses, see the liner notes to *Charley Patton: Founder of the Delta Blues* (Yazoo L1020), and Stephen Calt and Gayle Wardlow, *King of the Delta Blues* (Newton, NJ: Rock Chapel Press, 1988). Calt and Wardlow's book is often self-righteous and intemperate, containing full-scale assaults on other researchers (anachronistically labeled "Scholastics"), but it contains a wealth of helpful material on Patton. See especially Appendix 4, "Selected Songs." Patton's first name is more often spelled "Charley"—Paramount used that spelling in advertising his records—but Calt and Wardlow are not alone in preferring "Charlie."

21. Robert Johnson's lyrics are clearer than Patton's, but different listeners still hear different words. For transcriptions, see the liner notes for *Robert Johnson: The Complete*

Recordings (Columbia C2T 46222), and Samuel Charters, *Robert Johnson* (New York: Oak Publications, 1973). The best treatment of Johnson's life and career is Barry Lee Pearson and Bill McCulloch's *Searching for Robert Johnson* (Urbana: University of Illinois Press, 2003). Johnson's mention of Hot Springs in "32–20 Blues" is his own addition—when Skip James recorded the song (as "22–20 Blues") in 1931, the doctors were in "Wisconsin" (where the song was in fact recorded). That Johnson used James's version as his source is indicated by his restoration of "Wisconsin" when he repeated the stanza.

22. For a full account of Braswell's career as a composer and band organizer in Green Forest, Parthenon, and Jasper, see O. Klute Braswell, "The Stephen Foster of the Ozarks," *Carroll County Historical Society Quarterly* 24 (1979): 1–8.

23. Gene Fowler and Bill Crawford, *Border Radio* (Austin: Texas Monthly Press, 1987), 178, 87.

24. *Aunt Ollie Gilbert Sings Old Folk Songs to Her Friends* (Concord, AR: Rimrock [rlp 495], n.d.). "Go Wash in the Beautiful Stream" was collected in North Carolina in 1927–1928—see Newman Ivey White, ed., *North Carolina Folklore* (Durham, NC: Duke University Press, 1952), vol. III, 624.

25. For detailed discussions of early black gospel music, with emphasis on the work of Tindley, Campbell, and Dorsey, see Michael W. Harris, *The Rise of Gospel Blues: The Music of Thomas Andrew Dorsey in the Urban Church* (Oxford: Oxford University Press, 1992), and Bernice Johnson Reagon, ed., *We'll Understand It Better By and By: Pioneering African American Gospel Composers* (Washington, D.C.: Smithsonian Institution Press, 1992).

26. Information about Luther Presley comes from the Mary Hudgins collection in the Special Collections Division of the University of Arkansas Libraries. The Stamps Baxter biographical sketch is from Series 1, Folder 16, and is quoted with permission.

27. Charles K. Wolfe, "Gospel Music Goes Uptown: White Gospel Music, 1945–1955," in Ferris and Hart, eds., *Folk Music and Modern Sound,* 82. Wolfe also calls attention to the important role in gospel music recording played by the numerous independent record companies of the late 1940s. His list includes the President label, headquartered in Little Rock (85). The Special Collections division of the University of Arkansas Libraries in Fayetteville has a wonderful collection of songbooks and other materials related to white gospel music in the region gathered over many years by librarian/journalist Mary Hudgins of Hot Springs. I have made extensive use of this collection, and all information on Luther Presley and Floyd E. Hunter comes from materials gathered by Ms. Hudgins. A paper written by Dwight E. Hunter, Floyd's grandson, is especially interesting for its detailed portrait of the world of Arkansas singing schools and gospel conventions in the early decades of the twentieth century—it's titled "Arkansas Singin' School Teacher-Composer: Floyd E. Hunter" and found in the Hudgins collection, Series 1, Folder 9.

28. For surveys of black gospel music, see Anthony Heilbut, *The Gospel Sound: Good News and Bad Times* (New York: Harper and Row [Limelight Editions], 1987); Reagon, ed., *We'll Understand It Better By and By;* and Harris, *Gospel Blues.* For white gospel music, see Cusic, *The Sound of Light,* and Lois S. Blackwell, *The Wings of the Dove: The Story of Gospel Music in America* (Norfolk, VA: Donning, c. 1978). For Ira

Sankey, see Mel R. Wilhoit, "Ira Sankey: Father of Gospel Music," *Rejoice* 3 (1991): 9–16. For the Vaughan Music Company and other southern gospel publishers, see James D. Walbert, "James D. Vaughan and the Vaughan School of Music," *Rejoice* 2 (1990): 12–15. Information about Albert E. Brumley is from a songbook, *The Best of Albert E. Brumley* (Powell, MO: Albert E. Brumley and Sons, 1966) and from the program for the 1993 Albert E. Brumley Sundown to Sunup Gospel Sing. The Albert E. Brumley Sundown to Sunup Gospel Sing was held in Springdale for many years. Now it is held in Fayetteville at the University of Arkansas.

29. Humbard describes his family background and early career in his autobiography, *Put God on Main Street* (Akron, Ohio: Cathedral of Tomorrow, 1970). For discussion of the Cathedrals, see Cusic, *The Sound of Light,* 149–53.

30. The location of "Sadie Beck's plantation" was established with the help of many people, starting with Willard Gatewood and Jeannie Whayne at the University of Arkansas, who directed me to Oscar Fendler in Blytheville. Mr. Fendler sent me to Margaret Woolfolk in Marion, who told me Sadie Beck was the daughter of J. O. E. Beck, whose large plantation near Horseshoe Lake in southern Crittenden County also included holdings in Lee and St. Francis counties. Bobby Roberts also helped in this search by directing me to Caroline Cunningham at the West Helena Public Library. She told me Phillips County—my own first guess—was wrong, and suggested I look in the Hughes area of St. Francis County. That's when I saw Beck on the map, called Mr. Fendler, and closed in on Margaret Woolfolk, who told me all. Ms. Woolfolk's *A History of Crittenden County, Arkansas* (Marion, AR[?]: 1991) includes good material on music in the West Memphis area. See pages 314–15.

31. For biographical information about Lee Hays, see Doris Willens, *Lonesome Traveler: The Life of Lee Hays* (New York: Norton, 1988). For the Almanac Singers, see R. Serge Denisoff, *Great Day Coming: Folk Music and the American Left* (Urbana: University of Illinois Press, 1971), especially chapter 4, "The Almanac Singers." Denisoff also treats the Weavers, but does so briefly and with some unmerited condescension.

32. John A. Lomax, *Adventures of a Ballad Hunter* (New York: Macmillan, 1947), 147.

33. "The Rock Island Line," quoted in Norm Cohen, *Long Steel Rail: The Railroad in American Folksong* (Urbana: University of Illinois Press, 1981), 474.

34. Lomax, *Adventures of a Ballad Hunter,* 147. Several inconsistencies in the various accounts of "The Rock Island Line" should be noted. Where Lomax describes the song as accompanying cotton picking, Leadbelly calls it a wood-chopping song in his spoken introduction to his 1937 Library of Congress recording—his first recording of the song. Kelly Pace was released from prison in 1955 and died in 1958. Thanks to Mr. Otis Sams of Camden and Mr. and Mrs. Lawrence Pace of Bradley for help with information about Pace.

3 ✿ A Mixture Rich and Strange

1. Tosches, *Country,* 50–51.

2. Levon Helm and Stephen Davis, *This Wheel's on Fire: Levon Helm and the Story of the Band* (New York: William Morrow, 1993), 26, 27, 37.

3. The description of Phillips comes from Marion Keisker, his longtime assistant

and co-worker at Sun Records, as cited in Peter Guralnick, *Feel Like Going Home: Portraits in Blues and Rock 'n' Roll* (New York: Random [Vintage], 1981 [first published in 1971]), 172. The description of rockabilly is from Tosches, *Country,* pages 48–49. Similar sentiments are expressed by Greil Marcus in *Mystery Train: Images of America in Rock 'n' Roll Music* (New York: Dutton, 1976), 165: "Rockabilly was the only style of early rock 'n' roll that proved white boys could do it all—that they could be as strange, as exciting, as scary, and as free as the black men who were suddenly walking America's airwaves as if they owned them."

4. Colin Escott and Martin Hawkins, *Good Rockin' Tonight: Sun Records and the Birth of Rock 'n' Roll* (New York: St. Martin's Press, 1991), 51, 52. Another response to Hare's guitar work is available in Palmer, *Deep Blues,* 237–38. According to some reports, Hare shot not his baby but her husband.

5. The description by Bill Williams is from Peter Guralnick's lovely book, *Lost Highway: Journeys and Arrivals of American Musicians* (Boston: David R. Godine, 1979), 94–95. Sam Phillips's remark is from the same author's *Last Train to Memphis: The Rise of Elvis Presley* (Boston and New York: Little, Brown, 1994), 134.

6. Escott and Hawkins, *Good Rockin' Tonight,* 114, 186, 176. Escott and Hawkins are also my source for Sonny Burgess's birth date, though W. K. McNeil tells me he's seen newspaper interviews where Burgess reports a 1922 origin.

7. The "authorized" biography of Conway Twitty (so "authorized" that it omits his birth date) is *The Conway Twitty Story* by Wilbur Cross and Michael Kosser (New York: Doubleday, 1986). The description of Twitty City is from page 188. Cross and Kosser are even more coy in their handling of "You've Never Been This Far Before," "I'd Love to Lay You Down," "Slow Hand," and other soft-core "pornocountry" songs that were such hits for Twitty. These items are "not something dirty or risqué" at all, the problem comes when people read the lines "the way most males would." Twitty, on the other hand, was especially attuned to feminine sensibilities: "'Women understand how and why I select the songs I do,'" he said. "'They reach a point where they trust me to deal with their feelings and emotions'" (134).

8. For a thorough discussion of the Fordyce incident, see Chet Flippo, *On the Road with the Rolling Stones* (New York: Doubleday and Company, 1985), 53–55.

9. Chuck Cunning, *Fate Has Been My Friend: The Life and Times of Steve Stephens* (Hot Springs, AR: Alexus Publishing, 1998), 48.

10. Escott and Hawkins, *Good Rockin' Tonight,* 230.

11. Helm and Davis, *This Wheel's on Fire,* 62.

12. Information about The Browns comes from the reference work by Stambler and Landon cited in the bibliography. The Browns's 1959 album, *Sweet Sounds,* gave a name to the original 1996 exhibit.

13. I had a wonderful interview with Bob Boyd at his music store and studio in Little Rock on January 30, 1996.

14. Ed Ward, Geoffrey Stokes, and Ken Tucker, *Rock of Ages: The Rolling Stone History of Rock and Roll* (Englewood Cliffs, NJ: Rolling Stone Press [Prentice-Hall], 1986), 390.

15. I was guided to much information about Arkansas black gospel groups by Lee Anthony and his son Timothy Anthony. The Anthony family operates Soul Brother

Records in Little Rock, and Lee Anthony has for many years been active in managing and recording (on his True Soul and Gospel Showcase labels) area blues and gospel musicians.

16. Kenneth L. Smith, *Sawmill: The Story of Cutting the Last Great Virgin Forest East of the Rockies* (Fayetteville: University of Arkansas Press, 1986), 168. Smith treats the history of Forester in detail; photographs of Forester musicians appear on pages 177 (including Harry Standerfer) and 195.

17. "Forester (The Town That Moved Away)" was recorded by Griffith, once again backed by Glen Dale Sparks on bass, Roger Sparks on fiddle, Russell Sparks on banjo, and Lee Langston on guitar. The flip side is a narrative called "Forester Memories" by Dr. Vernon Carter. Dr. Carter was chairman of the Forester Historical Society; his father had operated the town's drugstore. The record was released on the ARK label based in Parks. Information on Forester comes from Smith, *Sawmill,* and from a research paper by Jennifer Mathis completed for my folk music course at the University of Arkansas in 1995.

18. I learned of both the Cryts ballad and of "Resurrection Sunday" from Vance Randolph and Gordon McCann, *Ozark Folklore: An Annotated Bibliography,* vol. II (Columbia: University of Missouri Press, 1987), 14, 19.

19. Deborah Robinson, "Singin' the Landfill Blues," *Northwest Arkansas Times,* January 22, 1996, 1.

Bibliography

General Reference Works

Claghorn, Charles Eugene. *Biographical Dictionary of American Music.* West Nyack, NY: Parker Publishing Company, 1973.

Clarke, Donald, ed. *The Penguin Encyclopedia of Popular Music.* New York: Viking, 1989.

Cohen, Norm. *Long Steel Rail: The Railroad in American Folksong.* Urbana: University of Illinois Press, 1981.

Cohen, Norm, ed. *Ozark Folksongs.* Urbana: University of Illinois Press, 1982.

DeCurtis, Anthony, and James Henke. *The Rolling Stone Album Guide.* New York: Random House, 1992.

Dixon, Robert M. W., and John Godrich. *Blues and Gospel Records, 1902–1942.* London: Storyville Publications, 1969.

Erlewine, Michael, Vladimir Bogdanov, and Chris Woodstra. *All Music Guide to Rock.* San Francisco: Miller Freeman Books, 1995.

Gammond, Peter. *The Oxford Companion to Popular Music.* Oxford: Oxford University Press, 1991.

Gentry, Linnell. *A History and Encyclopedia of Country, Western, and Gospel Music.* Nashville, TN: McQuiddy Press, 1961.

Hardy, Phil, and Dave Laing. *Encyclopedia of Rock.* New York: Schirmer Books (Macmillan), 1988.

Harris, Sheldon. *Blues Who's Who.* New Rochelle, NY: Arlington House, c. 1979.

Herzhaft, Gérard. *Encyclopedia of the Blues.* Fayetteville: University of Arkansas Press, 1992.

Hounsome, Terry. *Rock Record: A Collector's Directory of Rock Albums and Musicians.* New York: Facts on File, 1987.

Kernfeld, Barry, ed. *The New Grove Dictionary of Jazz.* London: Macmillan Press, 1988.

Kinkle, Roger D. *The Complete Encyclopedia of Popular Music and Jazz, 1900–1950.* New Rochelle, NY: Arlington House, 1974.

Knippers, Ottis J. *Who's Who among Southern Singers and Composers.* Lawrenceburg, TN: James D. Vaughan Music Publishers, 1937.

Larkin, Colin, ed. *The Guinness Encyclopedia of Popular Music.* Enfield, Middlesex, England: Guinness Publishing, 1992.

Lawless, Ray M. *Folksingers and Folksongs in America.* New York: Duell, Sloan and Pearce, 1960.

Leadbitter, Mike, and Neil Slaven. *Blues Records, 1943–1966: A Complete Guide to Twenty Years of Recorded Blues.* New York: Oak, 1968.

Malone, Bill C. *Country Music, U.S.A.* Austin: University of Texas Press, 1985 [revised edition].

McCloud, Barry. *Definitive Country.* New York: Berkley Publishing Group, 1995.

Murray, Charles Shaar. *Blues on CD: The Essential Guide.* London: Kyle Cathie, 1993.

Pebworth, James R. *A Directory of 132 Arkansas Composers.* Fayetteville: University of Arkansas Library, 1979.

Randolph, Vance. *Ozark Folksongs.* Columbia: University of Missouri Press, 1980 (first published 1946–1950).

Randolph, Vance, and Gordon McCann. *Ozark Folklore: A Bibliography.* Vol. II. Columbia: University of Missouri Press, 1987.

Sadie, Stanley, ed. *New Grove Dictionary of Music and Musicians.* Washington, D.C.: Grove Dictionaries of Music, 1980.

Smyth, Willie. *Country Music Recorded Prior to 1943: A Discography of LP Reissues.* Los Angeles, CA: John Edwards Memorial Forum, 1984.

Sonnier, Austin. *A Guide to the Blues: History, Who's Who, Research Sources.* Westport, CT: Greenwood Press, 1994.

Southern, Eileen. *Biographical Dictionary of Afro-American and African Musicians.* Westport, CT: Greenwood Press, 1982.

Stambler, Irwin, and Grelun Landon. *The Encyclopedia of Folk, Country and Western Music.* New York: St. Martin's Press, 1983.

White, Newman I., ed. *North Carolina Folklore.* Durham, NC: Duke University Press, 1952.

Other Works

Abrahams, Roger, ed. *A Singer and Her Songs: Almeda Riddle's Book of Ballads.* Baton Rouge: Louisiana State University Press, 1970.

Anonymous. "Bob 'Bazooka' Burns, The Arkansas Traveler, 1890–1956." Van Buren, AR: Van Buren Advertising and Promotion Commission, 1995.

Arnold, Morris S. *Colonial Arkansas, 1686–1804: A Social and Cultural History.* Fayetteville: University of Arkansas Press, 1991.

Arnold, Morris S. "Eighteenth-Century Arkansas Illustrated." *Arkansas Historical Quarterly* 53 (1994): 119–36.

Arnold, Morris S. "The Significance of Arkansas's Colonial Experience." In Jeannie Whayne, ed., *Cultural Encounters in the Early South: Indians and Europeans in Arkansas* (Fayetteville: University of Arkansas Press, 1995), 131–41.

Ault, Larry. "Arkansas Native, 'Silver Fox' Topped Country Charts in '70s." *Arkansas Democrat-Gazette,* July 26, 1995, 4.

Blackwell, Lois S. *The Wings of the Dove: The Story of Gospel Music in America.* Norfolk, VA: Donning, c1978.

Braswell, O. Klute. "The Stephen Foster of the Ozarks." *Carroll County Historical Society Quarterly* 24 (1979): 1–8.

Brown, Sarah. "'The Arkansas Traveler': Southwest Humor on Canvas." *Arkansas Historical Quarterly* 46 (1987): 348–75.

Brumley, Albert E. *The Best of Albert E. Brumley.* Powell, MO: Albert E. Brumley and Sons, 1966.

Buckalew, Terence H. *Blues Music in Arkansas.* Unpublished M.A. thesis, University of Arkansas, 1993.

Bufwack, Mary A., and Robert K. Oermann. *Finding Her Voice: The Saga of Women in Country Music.* New York: Crown, 1993.

Calt, Stephen, and Gayle Wardlow. *King of the Delta Blues: The Life and Music of Charlie Patton.* Newton, NJ: Rock Chapel Press, 1988.

Capaldi, Jim. "Wasn't That a Time!: A Conversation with Lee Hays." *Sing Out!* 28 (1981): 2–7.

Charters, Samuel. *Robert Johnson.* New York: Oak, 1973.

Chatto, James. "The Hawk Is 60." *Arkansas Times,* August 25, 1995, 7–8.

Chilton, John. *Let the Good Times Roll: The Story of Louis Jordan and His Music.* Ann Arbor: University of Michigan Press, 1994.

Clark, Ruby Neal, Mae Shull Holloway, Eleanor Bowling Ryman, and Alma Dean Stroud. *A History of Van Buren County, Arkansas, 1976.* Conway, AR: River Road Press, 1976.

Cochran, Robert. "'All the Songs in the World': The Story of Emma Dusenbury." *Arkansas Historical Quarterly* 44 (1985): 3–15.

Cochran, Robert. "Ride It Like You're Flyin': The Story of 'The Rock Island Line.'" *Arkansas Historical Quarterly* 56 (1997): 201–29.

Cochran, Robert. *Singing in Zion: Music and Song in the Life of an Arkansas Family.* Fayetteville: University of Arkansas Press, 1999.

Cohn, Lawrence, ed. *Nothing But the Blues: The Music and the Musicians.* New York: Abbeville Press, 1993.

Cooper, Daniel. *Lefty Frizzell: The Honky-Tonk Life of Country Music's Greatest Singer.* Boston: Little, Brown, 1995.

Cowley, John H. "Don't Leave Me Here: Non-Commercial Blues: The Field Trips, 1924–1960." In Lawrence Cohn, ed., *Nothing But the Blues: The Music and the Musicians* (New York: Abbeville Press, 1993), 264–311.

Cross, Wilbur, and Michael Kosser. *The Conway Twitty Story.* New York: Doubleday, 1986.

Cunning, Chuck. *Fate Has Been My Friend: The Life and Times of Steve Stephens.* Hot Springs, AR: Alexus Publishing, 1998.

Cusic, Don. *The Sound of Light: A History of Gospel Music.* Bowling Green, Ohio: Bowling Green State University Popular Press, 1990.

Dees, Jim. "Grits to Glory: Al Green Is Thy Valley." *Reckon* (1995): 124–26.

Delmore, Alton. *Truth Is Stranger Than Publicity: Alton Delmore's Autobiography.* Nashville, TN: Country Music Foundation Press, 1977.

Denisoff, R. Serge. *Great Day Coming: Folk Music and the American Left.* Baltimore, MD: Penguin, 1973.

DeWitt, Howard A. *Elvis, The Sun Years: The Story of Elvis Presley in the Fifties.* Ann Arbor, MI: Popular Culture, Ink, 1993.

Dixon, Robert M. W., and John Godrich. *Recording the Blues.* London: Studio Vista, 1970.

Dougan, Michael. *Arkansas Odyssey: The Saga of Arkansas from Prehistoric Times to the Present.* Little Rock, AR: Rose, 1994.

Dougan, Michael. *Confederate Arkansas: The People and Politics of a Frontier State in Wartime.* Tuscaloosa: University of Alabama Press, 1976.

Escott, Colin, with Martin Hawkins. *Good Rockin' Tonight: Sun Records and the Birth of Rock 'n' Roll.* New York: St. Martin's Press, 1991.

Featherstonhaugh, George W. *Excursion Through the Slave States.* London: John Murray, 1844.

Ferris, William, and Mary L. Hart, eds. *Folk Music and Modern Sound.* Jackson: University Press of Mississippi, 1982).

Flippo, Chet. *On the Road with the Rolling Stones.* Garden City, NY: Doubleday and Company, 1985.

Fowler, Gene, and Bill Crawford. *Border Radio.* Austin: Texas Monthly Press, 1987.

Gerstäcker, Friedrich. *Wild Sports in the Far West.* Durham, NC: Duke University Press, 1968.

Garon, Paul, and Beth Garon. *Woman with Guitar: Memphis Minnie's Blues.* New York: Da Capo Press, 1992.

Gilbert, Douglas. *American Vaudeville: Its Life and Times.* New York: Dover, 1963.

Goldstein, Kenneth S. "The Impact of Recording Technology on the British Folksong Revival." In William Ferris and Mary L. Hart, eds., *Folk Music and Modern Sound* (Jackson: University Press of Mississippi, 1982), 3–13.

Green, Archie. "Graphics #67: The Visual Arkansas Traveler." *John Edwards Memorial Foundation Quarterly* 21 (1985): 31–46.

Guralnick, Peter. *Feel Like Going Home: Portraits in Blues and Rock 'n' Roll.* New York: Random House, 1981.

Guralnick, Peter. *Last Train to Memphis: The Rise of Elvis Presley.* Boston: Little, Brown, 1994.

Guralnick, Peter. *Lost Highway: Journeys and Arrivals of American Music.* Boston: David Godine, 1979.

Guralnick, Peter. *Searching for Robert Johnson.* New York: E. P. Dutton, 1989.

Guralnick, Peter. *Sweet Soul Music: Rhythm and Blues and the Southern Dream of Freedom.* New York: Harper and Row, 1986.

Hamm, Charles. *Yesterdays: Popular Song in America.* New York: Norton, 1979.

Harrington, Mark R. *The Ozark Bluff-Dwellers.* New York: The Museum of the American Indian/Heye Foundation, 1971.

Harris, Michael W. *The Rise of Gospel Blues: The Music of Thomas Andrew Dorsey in the Urban Church.* Oxford: Oxford University Press, 1992.

Hawkins, Ronnie, and Peter Goddard. *Ronnie Hawkins: Last of the Good Ol' Boys.* Grawn, MI: Stoddart Publishing, 1990.

Hays, Sandy Miller. "Singer Bringing Wolverton Mountain to Wiederkehr Show." *Arkansas Democrat,* August 7, 1981, Weekend sec., 4.

Heilbut, Anthony. *The Gospel Sound.* New York: Limelight Editions, 1987.

Helm, Levon, with Stephen Davis. *This Wheel's on Fire: Levon Helm and the Story of the Band.* New York: William Morrow, 1993.

Hively, Kay, and A. E. Brumley Jr. *I'll Fly Away.* Branson, MO: Mountaineer Books, 1990.

Horse Capture, George P., Anne Vitart, and W. Richard West Jr. *Robes of Splendor: Native American Painted Buffalo Hides.* New York: New Press, 1993.

Hoskyns, Barney. *Across the Great Divide: The Band and America.* New York: Hyperion, c. 1993.

Hudgins, Mary. "A Musical Note on an Old Arkansas Song." *Arkansas Gazette,* September 25, 1966.

Humbard, Rex. *Put God on Main Street.* Akron, Ohio: Cathedral of Tomorrow, 1970.

Humphrey, Mark A. "Holy Blues: The Gospel Tradition." In Lawrence Cohn, ed., *Nothing But the Blues: The Music and the Musicians* (New York: Abbeville Press, 1993), 106–49.

Hutson, Kirk. "Hot 'n' Nasty: Black Oak Arkansas and Its Effect on Rural Southern Culture." *Arkansas Historical Quarterly* 54 (1995): 185–211.

Jackson, Jerma. *Singing in My Soul: Black Gospel Music in a Secular Age.* Chapel Hill: University of North Carolina Press, 2004.

Jernigan, Francis Hook. "Dr. Henry Harlin Smith, 1881–1931." *Izard County Historian* 5 (1974): 2–9.

Joutel, Henri. *The Last Voyage Perform'd by de la Sale.* Ann Arbor, MI: University Microfilms, 1966 [reprint of 1714 English edition].

Keefe, James F., and Lynn Morrow. *The White River Chronicles of S. C. Turnbo.* Fayetteville: University of Arkansas Press, 1994.

Lankford, George. "The Arkansas Traveler: The Making of an Icon." *Mid-America Folklore* lo (1982): 16–23.

Lindley, Helen C. "The Hoss-Hair Pullers and Hillbilly Quartet." *Izard County Historian* 5 (1974): 9–13.

Lomax, John. *Adventures of a Ballad Hunter.* New York: Macmillan, 1947.

Lottinville, Savoie, ed. *A Journal of Travels into the Arkansas Territory During the Year 1819, By Thomas Nuttall.* Norman: University of Oklahoma Press, 1980.

MacDonald, J. Fred. *Don't Touch That Dial!: Radio Programming in American Life, 1920–1960.* Chicago: Nelson-Hall, 1979.

McCulloh, Judith. "Uncle Absie Morrison's Historical Tunes." *Mid-South Folklore* 3 (1975): 95–104.

McDermott, John Francis, ed. *Tixier's "Travels on the Osage Prairies."* Norman: University of Oklahoma Press, 1940.

McKee, Margaret, and Fred Chisenhall. *Beale Black and Blue: Life and Music on Black America's Main Street.* Baton Rouge: Louisiana State University Press, 1981.

McNeil, W. K. "'By the Ozark Trail': The Image of the Ozarks in Popular and Folk Song." *John Edwards Memorial Foundation Quarterly* 21 (1985): 20–30.

McNeil, W. K. "Dr. Smith's Champion Horse-Hair Pullers: An Ozark String Band." *John Edwards Memorial Foundation Quarterly* 21 (1985): 120–26.

McNeil, W. K. "Five Pre–World War II Arkansas String Bands: Some Thoughts on Their Recording Success." *John Edwards Memorial Foundation Quarterly* 20 (1984): 68–75.

McNeil, W. K. *Southern Mountain Folksongs.* Little Rock, AR: August House, 1993.

Malone, Bill. *Singing Cowboys and Musical Mountaineers.* Athens: University of Georgia Press, 1993.

Malone, Bill, and Judith McCulloh. *The Stars of Country Music.* New York: Avon, 1976.

Marcus. Greil. *Mystery Train: Images of America in Rock 'n' Roll Music.* New York: Dutton, 1976.

Masterson, James. *Arkansas Folklore.* Little Rock, AR: Rose, 1974.

Melville, Herman. *Moby-Dick.* Evanston and Chicago: Northwestern University Press and The Newberry Library, 1988 (first published in 1851).

Morrison, Craig. *Go Cat Go!: Rockabilly Music and Its Makers.* Urbana: University of Illinois Press, 1996.

Nye, Russel. *The Unembarrassed Muse: The Popular Arts in America.* New York: Dial, 1970.

Palmer, Robert. *Deep Blues.* New York: Penguin, 1981.

Patterson, Ruth Polk. *The Seed of Sally Good'n: A Black Family of Arkansas, 1833–1953.* Lexington: University Press of Kentucky, 1980.

Pearson, Barry. "Jump Steady: The Roots of R&B." In Lawrence Cohn, ed., *Nothing But the Blues: The Music and the Musicians* (New York: Abbeville Press, 1992), 312–45.

Pearson, Barry, and Bill McCulloch. *Searching for Robert Johnson.* Urbana: University of Illinois Press, 2003.

Poindexter, Ray. *Arkansas Airwaves.* North Little Rock, AR: n.p., 1974.

Rainey, Leo. *Songs of the Ozark Folk.* Branson, MO: Ozarks Mountaineer, 1981.

Rawick, George P., ed. *The American Slave: A Composite Autobiography.* Westport, CT: Greenwood, 1972.

Read, Peter. "The Cate Brothers Band." *Nightflying,* Summertime Blues (1995): 6–8.

Reagon, Bernice Johnson. *We'll Understand It Better By and By: Pioneering African American Gospel Composers.* Washington, D.C.: Smithsonian Institution Press, 1992.

Rinne, Henry Q. "A Short History of the Alphonso Trent Orchestra." *Arkansas Historical Quarterly* 45 (1986): 228–49.

Robinson, Deborah. "Singin' the Landfill Blues." *Northwest Arkansas Times,* January 22, 1996, 1.

Rogers, Jimmie N. *The Country Music Message: Revisited.* Fayetteville: University of Arkansas Press, 1989.

Russell, Ross. *Jazz Style in Kansas City and the Southwest.* Berkeley: University of California Press, 1971.

Sabo, George. "Rituals of Encounter: Interpreting Native American Views of European Explorers." In Jeannie Whayne, ed., *Cultural Encounters in the Early South: Indians and Europeans in Arkansas* (Fayetteville: University of Arkansas Press, 1995), 76–87.

Schaffer, Archibald. "Cate Brothers: 35 Down and Plenty to Go!" Unpublished research paper, 1995.

Settel, Irving. *A Pictorial History of Radio.* New York: Bonanza Books, 1960.

Sloan, David. "The Expedition of Hernando DeSoto: A Post-mortem Report." In Jeannie Whayne, ed., *Cultural Encounters in the Early South: Indians and Europeans in Arkansas* (Fayetteville: University of Arkansas Press, 1995), 3–37.

Smith, Kenneth L. *Sawmill: The Story of Cutting the Last Great Virgin Forest East of the Rockies.* Fayetteville: University of Arkansas Press, 1986.

Spears-Stewart, Reta. *Remembering the Ozark Jubilee.* Springfield, MO: Stewart, Dillbeck & White Productions, 1993.

Spottswood, Richard K. "Country Girls, Classic Blues, and Vaudeville Voices: Women and the Blues." In Lawrence Cohn, ed., *Nothing But the Blues: The Music and the Musicians* (New York: Abbeville Press, 1993), 86–105.

Sutherland, Daniel, ed. *Reminiscences of a Private: William E. Bevens of the First Arkansas Infantry, C.S.A.* Fayetteville: University of Arkansas Press, 1992.

Thorpe, Thomas Bangs. "The Big Bear of Arkansas." In Walter Blair, ed., *Native American Humor* (Scranton, PA: Chandler, 1960).

Titon, Jeff Todd. *Early Downhome Blues.* Urbana: University of Illinois Press, 1977.

Tosches, Nick. *Country: The Biggest Music in America.* New York: Dell, 1977.

Tucker, Terry. "Cate Brothers' Southern Style Stings Rock World." *Springdale News,* April 21, 1976, 3.

Walbert, James D. "James D. Vaughan and the Vaughan School of Music." *Rejoice* 2 (1990): 12–15.

Wald, Elijah. *Escaping the Delta: Robert Johnson and the Invention of the Blues.* New York: Harper, 2004.

Ward, Ed, Geoffrey Stokes, and Ken Tucker. *Rock of Ages: The Rolling Stone History of Rock and Roll.* Englewood Cliffs, NJ: Prentice-Hall, 1986.

Whayne, Jeannie, ed. *Cultural Encounters in the Early South: Indians and Europeans in Arkansas.* Fayetteville: University of Arkansas Press, 1995.

White, Newman Ivey. *North Carolina Folklore.* Durham, NC: Duke University Press, 1952.

Wilhoit, Mel R. "Ira Sankey: Father of Gospel Music." *Rejoice* 3 (1991): 9–16.

Willens, Doris. *Lonesome Traveler: The Life of Lee Hays.* New York: Norton, 1988.

Williams, Leonard. "An Early Arkansas 'Frolic': A Contemporary Account." *Mid-South Folklore* 2 (1974): 39–42.

Wolf, John Quincy. *Life in the Leatherwoods: An Ozark Boyhood Remembered.* Little Rock, AR: August House, 1988.

Wolfe, Charles K. "Gospel Music Goes Uptown: White Gospel Music, 1945–1955." In William Ferris and Mary Hart, eds., *Folk Music and Modern Sound* (Jackson: University Press of Mississippi, 1982), 80–100.

Wolfe, Charles K., and Kip Lornell. *The Life and Legend of Leadbelly.* New York: Harper Collins, 1992.

Woolfolk, Margaret. *A History of Crittenden County, Arkansas.* Marion, AR[?]: Margaret Woolfolk, 1991.

Worley, Ted R., ed. *They Never Came Back: The War Memoirs of Captain John W. Lavender, C.S.A.* Pine Bluff, AR: W. M. Hackett and D. R. Perdue, c. 1956.

Wren, Christopher S. *Winners Got Scars Too: The Life and Legends of Johnny Cash.* New York: Dial Press, 1971.

INDEX

(Page numbers in bold indicate photographs. Arkansas towns are not identified by state; all other U. S. towns are [as are cities and countries abroad]. Thus "Philadelphia" is a small town in Arkansas, while "Dallas [Texas]" is a large town not in Arkansas; "England" is another small Arkansas town, while "Milan [Italy]" is a large Italian city.)

ROBERT COCHRAN is professor of English, chair of American Studies, and director of the Center for Arkansas and Regional Studies at the University of Arkansas. He is a Guggenheim Fellowship and Fulbright Lectureship winner, and the author of a number of books, including *Singing in Zion: Music and Song in the Life of an Arkansas Family*, *Samuel Beckett: A Study of the Short Fiction*, *Vance Randolph: An Ozark Life*, and *A Photographer of Note: Arkansas Artist Geleve Grice*.